FINANCE
AND
INFORMATION
A Study of
Converging Interests

COMMUNICATION AND INFORMATION SCIENCE

A series of monographs, treatises, and texts

Edited by

MELVIN J. VOIGT

University of California, San Diego

William C. Adams • Television Coverage of International Affairs

William C. Adams • Television Coverage of the Middle East

Hewitt D. Crane • The New Social Marketplace: Notes on Effecting Social Change in America's Third Century

Rhonda J. Crane • The Politics of International Standards: France and the Color TV War

Herbert S. Dordick, Helen G. Bradley, and Burt Nanus • The Emerging Network Marketplace

Glen Fisher • American Communication in a Global Society

Oscar H. Gandy, Jr. • Beyond Agenda Setting: Information Subsidies and Public Policy

Edmund Glenn • Man and Mankind: Conflict and Communication Between Cultures

Bradley S. Greenberg • Life on Television: Content Analyses of U.S. TV Drama

Robert M. Landau, James H. Bair, and Jean Siegman • Emerging Office Systems

John S. Lawrence and Bernard M. Timberg • Fair Use and Free Inquiry: Copyright Law and the New Media

Robert G. Meadow • Politics as Communication

William H. Melody, Liora R. Salter, and Paul Heyer • Culture, Communication, and Dependency: The Tradition of H.A. Innis

Vincent Mosco • Broadcasting in the United States: Innovative Challenge and Organizational Control

Vincent Mosco • Pushbutton Fantasies

Kaarle Nordenstreng and Herbert I. Schiller • National Sovereignty and International Communication: A Reader

Dan Schiller • Telematics and Government

Herbert I. Schiller • Who Knows: Information in the Age of the Fortune 500

Dallas W. Smythe • Dependency Road: Communications, Capitalism, Consciousness and Canada

Janet Wasko • Movies and Money: Financing the American Film Industry

In Preparation:

William C. Adams • Television Coverage of the 1980 Presidential Campaign

Mary Cassata and Thomas Skill • Life on Daytime Television: Tuning-In American Serial Drama

Ithiel de Sola Pool • Forecasting The Telephone: A Retrospective Technology Assessment

Bradley S. Greenberg • Mexican Americans and the Mass Media

Kaarle Nordenstreng • The Mass Media Declaration of UNESCO

Jorge A. Schnitman • Dependency and Development in the Latin American Film Industries

Indu B. Singh • Telecommunications in the Year 2000: National and International Perspectives

Jennifer D. Slack • Communication Technologies and Society: Conceptions of Causality and the Politics of Technological Intervention

Osmo Wiio • Information and Communication Systems

FINANCE AND INFORMATION
A Study of Converging Interests

Cees J. Hamelink
Institute of Social Studies, The Hague

ABLEX Publishing Corporation
355 Chestnut Street
Norwood, New Jersey 07648

Printed in the United States of America.

Library of Congress Cataloging in Publication Data

Hamelink, Cees, J., 1940-
  Finance and information.

  (Communication and information science)
  Bibliography: p.
  Includes indexes.
  1. Communication, International.   2. Communication—Economic
aspects.   3. International finance.   4. Communication—Social aspects.
I. Title.   II. Series.
P96.I5H34   001.51   81-17587
ISBN 0-89391-091-0   AACR2

ABLEX Publishing Corporation
355 Chestnut Street
Norwood, New Jersey 07648

This work was produced as part of the research programs of both the Division of Communication Studies and the Division of Economic Studies of the Latin American Institute of Transnational Studies (ILET) in Mexico City.

ILET is a non-governmental, non-profit international organization established in Mexico in 1976. Its basic subject of study is the transnational phenomena, in its economic, political and cultural dimension. Its aim is to promote a concept of Latin American Development oriented toward meeting the basic needs of the population, and based on real political participation and on the collective self-reliance of the region.

The author gratefully acknowledges the research support for this study by the Latin American Institute for Transnational Studies, Mexico City.

Table of Contents

List of Tables

List of Figures

Acknowledgement

The present study can be seen as a follow up to the earlier work I did for the publication entitled The Corporate Village (Rome, 1977). The theme of The Corporate Village was the role of transnational corporations in international communications. In dealing with the question of control I suggested the need for further exploration of the relationships between the information-industrial complex and its financiers.

The opportunity to collect and analyze more data on these relationships has been provided by the Latin American Institute for Transnational Studies (ILET) in Mexico. As member of the staff of the Institute I was charged with the execution of the research project on International Finance and International Communications. This was a joint project of the ILET Division of Communication Studies and the Division of Economic Studies. Throughout 1978 and 1979 the material and intellectual support from ILET helped the project well on its way. When I shifted base to the Institute of Social Studies in the Hague the project became also part of the ISS ongoing research. During 1980 the project could be finished with the support of the staff and facilities of the Institute of Social Studies.

The completed study now in front of you aspires by no means to be the last word on this nagging question of the control over international communications. It is a contribution to an important debate; a contribution that is meant to inspire others to further exploration.

For their contributions to the collecting of data and their comments on earlier versions of the manuscript acknowledgements are due to the following persons: Stephen Abrecht, Robert B. Cohen, Henry Ergas, Peter Golding, Noreene Janus, Gerd Junne, Aart J. M. van de Laar, Michael Locker, Graham Murdock, Russel G. Pipe, Fernando Reyes Matta, Rafael Roncagliolo, Herbert I. Schiller, Juan Somavia, Raùl Trajtenberg, Constantine Vaitsos, Richard H. Veith.

Special mention for their helpful assistance deserves the New York based research group Corporate Data Exchange.

Cees J. Hamelink
ILET, Mexico
ISS, the Hague
May 15, 1981.

Preface

This book on "Finance and Information" was written as part of the research programme of the Latin American Institute for Transnational Studies (ILET). Since it was founded in 1976, ILET has concentrated its research on the economic and communication aspects of the transnational power structure which pervades and controls developing countries. Within this line of research, Hamelink's book describes the complex bonds which link information enterprises to transnational banks. This analysis reveals the contemporary information systems as a major link to the financial sector and to the world-wide process of transnationalization. An important aspect of this book is the emphasis on the social consequences of current technological processes, an emphasis which characterizes the new four-year period (1981-1984) of research activities at ILET.

This new area of research interest is perfectly consistent with recent developments in the international debate on the New International Information Order as a result of the McBride Commission Report and the UNESCO General Conference in Belgrade in 1980. In fact, the first round of the debate, starting with the 1973 Algiers meeting of Heads of States on Governments of Non-Aligned countries, centered on the problems of the "free flow of information". This concept which, as has been convincingly demonstrated, consisted of a unilateral and quasi-monopolistic flow of news on an international level. Today, after the McBride Report and the Belgrade Conference, it is vitally important to draw attention to other equally important information flows: private data flows between giant enterprises and banks.

In the history of communication, the 80's will be looked back upon as the breakthrough of the world-wide diffusion of digital telecommunication. This type of communication technology has facilitated the homogenization of all existing forms of information and a speed and efficiency of transmission heretofore unknown. Furthermore, however, it has generated a qualitatively different kind of information.

This technological development—apart from its potential uses in the peripheral world—responds mainly to the interests and needs of the multinational system in both military as well as politico-economical areas. These sectors are well aware that telematics helps the major international powers and their allies to strengthen mechanisms of social control. Therefore, the study of the socio-political implications of this kind of technology is an urgent task for ILET. This book is an important step in the study of a crucial phenomenon of the commercial use of telematics: the private data flows of giant multinational enterprises.

Transnational information enterprises include not only the mass media and production for mass media but basic computer services, hardware manufacturers and software companies, those enterprises which buy and sell information and those which operate data processing and transmission systems. Owing to the high costs of production—particularly in terms of investments required by research and development—such transnational information enterprises require increasingly large financial investments which, in turn, makes them increasingly dependent on the transnational financial system.

Transnational banks, on the other hand, depend increasingly on electronic, and particularly on telematic forms of communications to handle their large volumes of transactions at a global level. They require this equipment not only to increase the speed of their financial transactions locally and world-wide, but also to develop investment alternatives and to provide vital information relating to political analysis, profits and investments at an international level, personal and business credit information, etc. Thus, transnational banks are among the most important users of data communication networks (S.W.I.F.T., EUREX, etc.), and, therefore the control of international information infrastructures and resources acquires great strategic significance.

A central question brought up in this study is: Who controls the information infrastructure and resources? Apart from this main question, the author makes the distinction between "operational control", which for example the editor-in-chief of a newspaper or a television station has, and "allocative control", meaning the control which determines the structure, the organization of industrial resources, product lines, division of labor and management policies.

The increasing concentration of allocative control over global information resources is facilitated by the structures integrating the information industry and the transnational financial system.

Financial organizations become increasingly dependent on the availability of data banks which are capable of providing instantly complete and up-to-date files of world-wide information related to investment alternatives. These computerized systems not only take into consideration classical economic variables, but also information relating to political stability, socio-economic policies of governments, characteristics of the opposition and general cultural aspects on a day-to-day basis.

This flow of private information tends to replace the mass of information which until now has been available through publicly accessible information sources (newspapers, news broadcasts, etc.). In other words, the financial system increasingly relies on its own internal information and communication systems to provide it with global information, systematized according to its particular interests.

The difference between "news" and "information", suggested by transnational representatives, refers in fact to the potential existence of two flows of information. On the one hand, the flow of information essential to decision-making circulates primarily through private channels controlled by transnational financial forces and, on the other hand, the "news", as it is traditionally defined, is presented to the public through the mass media. In this way, the general information system including the mass media, is open and accessible to all, but it comprises only a part of the global flows—precisely the least important part, the most crisis focused, and the most fragmented and removed from context. Given this perspective, the computerized society implies an increasing polarization between a small number of business groups with huge concentrated information capacities for decision-making and an uninformed majority which only has access to the "news" level. Undoubtedly this increase in private information flows not only promotes a growing privatization of decision-making but also facilitates socio-political manipulation based on the divorce between public and private information channels.

It has been argued that the new information technology—particularly telematics—may provide private citizens in their home with the possibility of accessing data banks on an individual basis, thus "democratizing" access to information for broad strata of society. However, one must also ask if these private computerized information systems will transform the domi-

nant concept of news (or in the new differentiation between news and information) as well as the role of gate-keepers, this time not for the press but
rather for data banks.

These private information flows have important implications for the
relationship between the government and the private sector. Even when a
certain level of control over communications is attained by governments,
these private flows can remain outside of the scope of such control and even
allow decisions to be made disregarding governmental policies. That is to
say, there are certain types of decisions on national affairs which in many
cases are of a strategic importance and which can be taken even without the
knowledge and control of governmental sectors. Undoubtedly these and
other aspects or private information flows affect national sovereignty in a
decisive way, and at the same time have complex consequences for national
states which themselves are clients of the transnational corporations.

The bank-information industry complex forms the nervous system of
the transnational power structure where private information flows acquire
a strategic importance of such magnitude that it cannot be ignored in any
debate on the New International Information Order (NIIO) or the New International Economic Order (NIEO). At the same time it emphasizes the in-
timate relation which exists between the NIIO and the NIEO. Thus, it is
increasingly important to analyze the various points of convergence of both
proposals especially since it is clear that the debate on a New World Order
can not afford to ignore those factors which appear as central power nuclei
of the present situation. Should the NIIO restrict itself solely to improve-
ments at the level of information flows related to the mass media, it will be
ignoring one of the central pillars: a vital part of the world-wide information
flows.

Efforts to legislate limits or controls on public information flows are
often opposed under the banner of "a free flow of information". Yet these
public information flows tend to be less important in relative terms (even
though they continue to be essential for political and cultural aspects of the
transnational system) as compared to private information flows which are
now of vital importance for the operations of transnational financial
systems. At the same time, as it is increasingly difficult to differentiate
various types of information—news or political information becomes at the
same time financial information—legislation on the control over information flows will most likely encounter powerful opposition and strong resis-
tance from transnational corporations and banks.

Thus, an arena of confrontation takes shape which is of vital importance for the determination of the final fate of the NIEO and of the NIIO.
ILET hopes that this and further research within the same field will con-

tribute to the rational and systematic knowledge of the new phenomenon and thereby to the process of achieving genuine and complete emancipation for Third World nations.

Rafael Roncagliolo, *Director*
Division of Communication Studies
ILET
Mexico City, July 1981

1

On Information
and Power

"It used to be that a person could live isolated from the world's problems,"
Lucy mused the other day. "Then it got to be that we all knew everything that
was going on. The problem now", she tells Snoopy, "is that we know
everything about everything except what's going on."

THE INFORMATION ECONOMY

When the electric movement of words was accomplished in 1844
Samuel Morse transmitted this legendary sentence "What has God wrought."
A little over a century later his exclamation still seems very appropriate
when reviewing the growth, scope, and impact of international telecommunications.

The history of communications is characterized by efforts to expand
the ingenious systems that human beings designed for the imparting and
receiving of information in face-to-face relations. Early in history man felt a
need to broaden the human facilities upon which such systems were based.
Thus commenced an ongoing search for "extensions" with which information could be carried over distances (tele). Among the first of these extensions
was the smoke signal. It enabled the transmitting of information over great
distances, but with evident limitations; the volume of messages that could

1

be communicated was restricted and weather conditions brought serious handicaps.

In fact the red thread throughout telecommunications history is the desire to overcome such restrictions and to make the communication of information possible over ever longer distances, in larger volumes, at higher speeds, and with greater reliability.

The first phase of *non-electric telecommunications* saw a variety of complex signalling systems, such as the flags that were used in the 17th century Dutch-British wars, or the semaphore invented by the Chappe brothers and applied during the Napoleonic wars by the British army as an alarm system, or the 19th century carrier-pigeons of Julius Reuters' international news service.[1] These systems had little differentiation in the messages that could be transported, suffered from dependence upon the weather. With bad weather communication was hardly possible, and information could be carried over relatively short distances.

In the second phase of telecommunications' history: the *electric transfer of information*, some of the limitations were overcome. The electric telecommunication systems (telephone, telex, radio, television) are a significant development towards optimal extensions. Most decisive, however, will be the third phase, upon which telecommunications definitely embarks in the 1980s: *digital telecommunications.*[2]

In this phase all the traditionally distinct media used for information transfer (such as telex), information storage (such as paper), and information processing (such as the human brain) converge into one medium: the computer network. The one carrier for all types of information will be the digital signal. All information flows will become digital data flows, and consequently the enormous capacity of the electronic computer can be applied to any type of information traffic. The implication is that enormous quantities can be transported very reliably and at extremely high speeds. The concept of distance has finally lost its meaning.[3]

Telecommunications' third phase coincides with the time when most industrialized nations enter the "information economy." The collecting, processing, and transmitting of information has become a major industrial activity, engaging increasing percentages of the labor force and yielding growing percentages of gross national products. As Marc Porat analyzed in a report for the U.S. Department of Commerce, "By 1977 we are just on the edge of becoming an information economy. The information technologies —computers and telecommunications—are the main engines of this transformation. And we are now seeing the growth of new information industries, products, services and occupations."[4]

At the heart of this development, as Porat rightly points out, are two information technologies and, more precisely, their convergence into what the French call "telematique" and what is by some referred to as "compunications."[5] This is the vital factor in what Nora and Minc describe as "l'informatisation de la société."[6]

In the socalled industrialized societies the processing of raw data into information plays an ever more central role. This means that there is a development from a society in which agriculture was the center of economic activity, via the industrial economy, to a situation in which the producing, processing, storing, and distributing of information becomes the key economic activity. This implies that in the different sectors of the economy a considerable number of people are engaged with informational activities. In 1976 the West German economy, for example, showed the following picture:

Sectors of the Economy	% of Jobs Related to Information
Industrial Production	24
Construction	14.4
Transportation/Utility	52.9
Trade	37.2
Finance/Insurance	80.1
Public Administration	49.1

(Source: S. Wall, Growth data of the information industry and the problems of measuring information activities and commodities; document for the OECD Working Party on Information, Computer and Telecommunication Policy, Paris, February 1979.)

As early as the end of the 1950s the classical core industries, such as textile, steel, rubber, and automotive, began to lose their meaning and have been increasingly replaced by new industries, such as electronics, aerospace, biochemistry, and the exploitation of the seas. These are all industries in which information is an essential and characteristic element.

As industrial production processes increase in complexity, the importance of information increases greatly. The manufacturing of simple products requires large amounts of labor force, material, and manual skill, but relatively little information. This changes with the production of more complicated machinery, with information becoming increasingly significant in relation to labor and material. More and more production processes have in fact become information processes (cf. the application of industrial robots).

Much of the costs of industrial production can be seen as information costs. These include costs of research and development, market exploration, and advertising. Also, the internationalization of industrial production demands more information traffic, the geographically spread units of transnational corporations have to be coordinated through elaborate information networks. Today a large corporation with sales of $1 billion will spend some 14 million dollars on telecommunications alone.[7]

Management of industrial production has become largely the collecting, processing, and transmitting of information. It has been estimated that managers of large corporations spend 80% of their time performing 200 to 300 information acts daily.[8]

In the shift towards the information economy the role of the so-called services sector of the economy is essential. Many of its activities (in banking, administration, telecommunications, etc.) are in fact related to the processing of information. This sector contributes more to the Gross National Product in the U.S., Canada, Japan, and several Westeuropean countries than the combined agricultural and industrial sectors. This is also the case in the countries that are usually referred to as "the newly industrialising countries." Many of them, in fact, are on their way of becoming information economies (see table).

Contribution Services Sector to the Economy (1976)

Country	Distribution GNP in %		
	Agriculture	Industry	Services
Korea	27	34	39
Mexico	10	35	55
Brazil	8	39	52
Hong Kong	2	34	64
Greece	18	31	51
Singapore	2	35	63
Spain	9	39	52

(Source: World Development Indicators, World Bank).

Lastly, it must be mentioned that the large service economy countries have a highly developed "information industry." This industry encompasses the corporations that produce and distribute information goods and services, such as newspapers, radio/TV programs, records, books, advertising, and consumer electronics. This information industry has a rapidly growing significance in both the domestic and the international economy.

In the U.S. economy, for example, the activities of the information industry are considered to be crucial in terms of the economic survival.[9] In worldwide trade the contribution of the computer and telecommunications industry alone amounts to some 10% in 1980. U.S. exports in this field have increased 2–3 times between 1972 and 1977. Between 1965 and 1975 the share of information goods and services in exports from OECD countries increased from 13% to 20%.[10] As an OECD report analyzes, the increased economic significance of information activities has had three major impacts on international economic relations. "First, it has stimulated international trade in several new information-related goods and services, while at the same time increasing international demand for the more mature information-related product lines. Second, it has given rise to international investment activity in information-related industries, particularly those involving new products and services. And, third, it has encouraged particularly in the electronics sector—the formation of a network of technology transfers linking firms in different countries through licensing agreements and patent exchange."[11] Regarding the second type of impact, the economic dimension of the information industry has indeed attracted the attention of large transnational corporations that formerly had little or no operations in the informational area and, in recent years, decided to move in. Some examples are: an oil company—Exxon, with Exxon Information Systems encompassing fifteen computer firms, such as Periphonics, in 1979 among the largest U.S. datacommunications equipment manufacturers; an aircraft manufacturer— Boeing with Boeing Computer Service Company, a $96 million computer services operation (in 1979) for commercial customers; a French building materials and metal products giant—Saint Gobain-Pont-à-Mousson, with 10% stock of CII-Honeywell Bull and one-third control of Olivetti, thus linking two important computer firms; an automobile manufacturer—Volkswagen, with almost three-quarters control of the mini- and microcomputer producer Triumph-Adler; a French missile and electronics manufacturer— Matra, which acquired 51% of the stock of publishing firm Hachette in December 1980.[12]

INFORMATION AND POWER

The use of the concept "information economy" in the present study should not be interpreted as a post-industrial perspective in which advanced information technology is expected to revolutionize the relations of power in society. What is meant here is that in advanced capitalism the distribution and execution of social power is increasingly related to the resource information.

With reference to Francis Bacon's thesis that "knowledge is power" information is often equated with power. This is, however, a deceptive notion. Whether the possession of information indeed enables access to the execution of social power depends upon a series of conditions. Information implies access to social power if its proprietor has access to the raw material of information (data), to the infrastructures for the processing of information, and to the social networks for the application of information to decision-making.

Access to the raw material of information is not decisive per se. In principle, most actors in society could gain access to a profusion of data that would still not increase their social power. Data have obviously to relate in a pertinent manner to social decision-making. It is therefore crucial to have the analytical skill to detect exactly the pertinent data. This is facilitated if one can handle massive quantities of data and search through them with electronic intelligence.

The case of remote earth resources sensing through photo satellites provides the clear illustration. Oil companies, for example, have access to data on resource locations and similarly to the expertise needed to assess the pertinence of gathered data. Another important factor in the access to the raw material is its timing. Early access in advance of others is an evident advantage as banker Nathan Rothschild knew when he organized his private carrier pigeon service. Through this he obtained early data on Napoleon's defeat at Waterloo (1815) and was able to take stock market decisions before his competitors and conduct profitable transactions with British state securities. The president of the GeoSat Committee has testified to the importance of early access through remote sensing: "The United States cannot afford to lose the remaining advantages that have come from developing technologies that have allowed us to become primary finders and developers of the world's non-renewable resources."[13]

The case of remote sensing also illustrates the importance of the access to infrastructures: the equipment and analytical skill needed for processing the data into applicable information. Having access to such infrastructures enables an oil company to use the satellite data "for locating prime uranium targets, laying out pipeline routes through mountains, extra-polating geologic models to upgrade offshore drilling locations, pinpointing hot spots of concern in our refineries, mapping ancient burnout zones in coal fields, predicting areas of intensely fractured rocks for safety control in mining and . . . preliminary oil and gas exploration."[14]

Access to the raw material and its analyzed format does not necessarily imply access to its application in decision-making. Additionally access is needed to the social networks through which information can be applied. Such networks are constituted through a variety of interlocks between social groups and individuals. As research on community decision-making shows the alliance with powerful groups and individuals determines the impact of the information that various social actors hold.[15]

The foregoing observations can be summed up as the point of departure for the present study: in advanced capitalism the distribution and execution of social power is increasingly related to the capacity to control the resource information through the access to its raw material, to the infrastructures for its processing and to the social networks for its application in decision-making.

DISPARITIES IN CAPACITY

A growing body of research evidence points to the existence of large disparities in the capacity to control the resource information.[16] The differential access to the collecting and analyzing of data and to the mobilization of networks for the application of information has created serious political concern.

International organizations, such as UNESCO, and academic circles in both developed and Third World countries have collected a substantial body of evidence supporting the thesis that current international information structures promote dependence between nations, legitimize existing economic disparities, and contribute to the cultural synchronization of the world.[17] The so-called "free flow of information" does not facilitate a diverse and open exchange of information between independent nations, with sovereign expressions of their economic and cultural systems.

The international flow of information has not brought about the "global village" in which everyone knows everything that's going on. Instead the village has been inundated with messages that tell "everything about everything except what's going on."

This situation confronts us with a host of problems. How well informed are we really about the events that shape the world's agenda, and their structural backgrounds? What is the role of all information flowing point-to-point within private networks escaping any form of public accountability? How well can a nation protect the information privacy of its own citizens? Who has privileged access to decisive types of specialized technical and scientific information?

Throughout the 1970s Third World countries at various fora have expressed their rejection of the current neo-colonial structure in international information traffic. Their position has come to be conceptualized in the call for a new international information order. Challenges have come also from another perspective; from those protagonists of informational freedom who feared that the disequilibrium in information control and content could defeat free flow itself. U.S. authorities have worried increasingly about cartelization in the information industry, for example, the U.S. Justice Department and its concern about the formation of trusts in the film indus-

try. At a symposium of the U.S. Federal Trade Commission on media concentration (December 14–15, 1978) several witnesses assailed the lack of
media diversity as a result of the alarming levels that media concentration
had reached. At the symposium Senator Larry Pressler said, "A Teddy
Roosevelt era of trust busting is needed to break up the media giants."
Because, as Ben Bagdikian (former Washington Post editor) claimed, "Fewer
than 100 corporate executives have ultimate control of the majority of each
medium in the United States." FTC chairman Michael Pertschuk analyzed,
"We must examine whether the right of free speech can be dissociated from
the economic structure of the media which give access to that speech . . . The
First Amendment protects us from the chilling shadow of government inter-
ference with the media. But are there comparable dangers if other powerful
economic or political institutions assume control of the media."[18] The same
question was phrased in a different way by P. Dreier and S. Weinberg in a
contribution to the *Columbia Journalism Review,* where they expressed
concern about the independent nature of U.S. journalism. They had found
in their research that "most of the 290 directors of the 25 largest newspaper
companies are tied to institutions the papers cover."[19] Similarly, the August
15, 1977 issue of US News & World Report asked on its front cover, "America's Press—too much power for too few?" As the accompanying article
commented, "There is growing concern that the publishing business, long
considered essential to an informed citizenry, is losing its diversity and that
growth of corporate empires in publishing is making the bottom line of
profit margins the supreme factor in the industry—to the detriment of ex-
cellence and responsibility to the public."[20]

Equally concerned about the impact of this phenomenon on the international scale was the International Commission for the Study of Communication Problems (the so-called MacBride Commission). In its UNESCO
sponsored report, the Commission observed that, "Concentration of resources and infrastructures is not only a growing trend, but also a worrying
phenomenon which may adversely affect the freedom and democratization
of communication."[21]

As Gabriel Garcia Marquez and Juan Somavia have stated in their
comment on the report, "More democratic communication structures are a
national and international need of peoples everywhere. Promoting access,
participation, decentralization, open management, and the diffusion of the
power concentrated in the hands of commercial or bureaucratic interests, is
a worldwide necessity."[22]

The MacBride report has pointed to important barriers in the way of
this democratization. One among them is particularly pertinent for the
present study, "the transnationalization of the production, financing, and

marketing of communication." As the report rightly observed, "This process has reached such proportions that transnationalization has become in many countries a factor largely, if not wholly, beyond the control of the policy-makers."[23]

THE ALLOCATIVE CONTROLLERS

The foregoing brings up the most crucial question of present-day international relations: where is the capacity to control the resource information located? The concern here is not with the daily operational type of control that influences informational goods and services on the level of the newspaper editor, the advertising designer, or the film director. More fundamentally, the *allocative type of control* is at stake, control that influences the scope, structure, and organization of industrial resources, lines of production, labor division, and management personnel policy. In search of the *"capacitating structure"* that facilitates allocative control over global information resources and infrastructures, the present study focuses on two key institutions of advanced capitalism and their interlocks: the information industry and the banking industry.

This is not an incidental choice. The international banking system plays a considerable role in the allocation of the world's financial resources and—as will be shown later—is heavily involved in the exploitation of the resource information. The information industry—as will also be shown later—is on various levels interlocked with the banking system. The information industry is responsible for most of the world's information processing and is in control of the majority of production and distribution structures. As Raymond Williams has observed, "The major modern communications systems are now so evidently key institutions in advanced capitalist societies that they require the same kind of attention, at least initially, that is given to the institutions of industrial production and distribution."[24]

The present study will explore in how far the interests of the information industry and the banking system converge and whether such convergence of interests renders them the allocative controllers of the resource information.

SUMMARY

The point of departure for the present study is the observation that in advanced capitalism the distribution and execution of social power is increasingly related to the control over the resource information. The capacity for such control is unevenly divided among the actors in society. This hinders the establishment of democratic communication processes.

The study explores in how far the interests of two key institutions of advanced capitalism: the information industry and the banking system are interlocked. If a convergence of interests can be established, the study questions whether this creates the capacitating structure for the allocative control over the resource information.

NOTES TO CHAPTER 1

[1] This semaphore was constructed as a pole with sidearms. The corner between pole and arms created by certain positions of the arms represented the code signal. With the semaphore used on the British Southcoast and along the way to London 192 messages could be sent.

[2] Information can be transported in the form of analogous or digital signals. In the analogous transfer the electrical signal represents the information that is to be transmitted. If the sound, for example, is strong, the signal is strong: it is analogous with its origin. This precise representation has to be maintained even over great distances. This can easily be distorted. In digital transfer the information is transmitted through series of binary digits (zeros and ones). This makes the transfer less vulnerable to distortion.

[3] Ed. F. M. Hogrebe, "Dangers and Opportunities of Digital Communication Media," Report for ILET, Mexico City, April 1980.

[4] M. U. Porat, *The Information Economy*, Study for the U.S. Department of Commerce/Office of Telecommunications, May 1977, Vol. I, p. 204.

[5] The term "compunications" was coined by the Harvard University Program on Information Resources Policy.

[6] S. Nora and A. Minc, *L'Information de la Société*. La documentation francaise, Paris, 1978.

[7] W. N. Barnes (v.p. Collins Communications Switching Systems of Rockwell International) in *Fortune*, January 28, 1980.

[8] A. Toffler, *The Third Wave*, Morrow, New York, 1980, p. 203.*

* H. Mintzberg in *The Nature of Managerial Work*, Harper L. Row, New York, 1973, has calculated that corporate managers spend $\frac{1}{3}$–$\frac{1}{2}$ of the time on face-to-face meetings, $\frac{1}{4}$–$\frac{1}{3}$ of the time on written communications (memos, letters and reports) and a good deal of the remaining time on telephone calls.

[9] Cf. for example a statement by the National Association of Manufacturers (in the U.S.) in a letter to the Chairman of the House Subcommittee on Government Information and Individual Rights, "The indications are that the information technology sector will be critical for the United States as it faces the intensely competitive world economic situation for the 80's. Our world leadership in this field will benefit American trade directly, through the export of goods and services in this sector itself, and

indirectly through improving the competitive efficiency of U.S. companies worldwide in all sectors," March 1980.

[10] From: "The Role of Information Goods and Services in International Trade," A working paper prepared for the OECD working party on Information, Computer and Communications Policy, Paris, May 1979.

[11] Ibid.

[12] In addition to the 51% share held by Matra, the BanquePrivée de Gestion Financière holds 19%, the Banque de Paris et des Pays Bas holds 10%, and the Groupe Fillipachi 20%.

Matra has in recent years already diversified into radio (Europe 1), television (Tele Monte Carlo), satellites, telematics sets (for the French video telephone book due by 1990), and press (20 Ans, Jacinte, Biba).

[13] F. B. Henderson during Hearings before the Subcommittee on Science, Technology and Space of the Committee on Commerce, Science and Transportation of the U.S. Senate, July 31, 1970.

[14] Quoted by H. I. Schiller in "Planetary Resource Information Flows: A New Dimension of Hegemonic Powe or Global Social Utility?". Paper for the Conference World Communications: Decisions for the Eighties, Annenberg School of Communications, Philadelphia, May 1980.

[15] Cf. J. E. Grunig, "Communication in Community Decisions on the Problems of the Poor", In *The Journal of Communication*, vol. 22, March 1972, pp. 5-25.

[16] Much of the research in this field has been compiled in the Report of the UNESCO sponsored International Commission for the Study of Communication Problems, *Many Voices, One World*, UNESCO, Paris, 1980. In particular: Part II chapter 6 and Part III, chapter 1.

[17] C. J. Hamelink, *Cultural Autonomy in Global Communications*, Longman, New York, 1982.

[18] Editor & Publisher, Dec. 23, 1978.

[19] P. Dreier and S. Weinberg, "Interlocking Directorates", *Columbia Journalism Review*, Nov./Dec. 1979, pp. 51-68.

[20] A. P. Sarnoff, "America's Press: Too Much Power for Too Few?", *U.S. News & World Report*, Aug. 15, 1977, p. 27.

[21] International Commission for the Study of Communication Problems, *Many Voices, One World*, UNESCO, Paris, 1980, p. 111.

[22] Ibidem, p. 281.

[23] Ibidem, p. 212.

[24] R. Williams, *Marxism and Literature*, Oxford University Press, Oxford, 1977, p. 136. The key position of the information industry is a.o. related to its technology and the dual function thereof: as a means of production and as an instrument of social control. Cf. a comment by F. de Benedetti, managing director of Olivetti, "...it is in fact an organizational technology and, like the organization of labour, has a dual function: as a productive force and a control tool for capital." (In the paper "The Impact of Electronic Technology in the Office", Conference: Tomorrow in World Electronics, London, March 1979.

2

The Importance
of Finance
for the
Information Industry

THE TRANSNATIONAL
INFORMATION-INDUSTRIAL COMPLEX

This chapter describes the transnational information industry in its overall scope, identifies its various sectors and their interlocks, analyzes its transnationalization, its rate of concentration, and its capital intensity.

The point of departure for this study is a comprehensive look at the totality of the production and distribution of informational goods and services. The usual restriction of the debate on information-communication issues to "mass media" structures and contents is deliberately avoided as a distorting limitation in the analysis of the international mechanisms that are gatekeeping one of the world's vital resources.

This makes it necessary to describe the transnational production and distribution of informational goods and services in its total volume and also to subdivide it into meaningful sub-categories.

The broad scope of the study aims at including in the analysis all those institutions and actors involved in the collecting, processing, and distributing of information's raw material: data.

In order to use a term that both characterizes the totality and its sub-categories the generic concept "information" will be used. This makes it possible to look not only at what is customarily described as "communication media," but also at data processing, datacommunications, and various forms of supporting hardware. The production and distribution of information goods and services thus encompass: the manufacturing of the *technical equipment* through which a variety of different forms of information processing and transmitting takes place, the producing and selling of *information as a commodity*, and the *operating of systems* through which information can be processed and/or transmitted.

A difficulty that must be noted at the beginning is the collecting of accurate figures on the information industry. As C. Sterling and T. Haight indicate in the introduction to their guide for communication industry trends, "The overall question of 'Who controls the media and to what degree?' cannot really be answered with available statistics. For many communication industries, information is scarce."[1]

And as N. Garnham states for one of the industry's sectors, "The difficulty of obtaining accurate financial data is notorious among those who have studied the U.S. film industry."[2] A similar difficulty is encountered in the data-processing industry, "It is impossible to follow the changing picture of the world computer market; with any real degree of accuracy."[3]

Moreover, a complication is that many corporations do not separate their financial figures by product category and provide overall figures only.

Despite these very real difficulties, the following pages will try to provide the maximum possible degree of insights into volume and scope of international information production and distribution. This has certain consequences for the dating of the figures used. For overall comparisons it was necessary to go back to 1976, whereas in several individual cases more recent information could be used.

TRANSNATIONAL INFORMATION CORPORATIONS

In an earlier study I identified the 81 transnational corporations that could be held accountable for the production and distribution of some 75% of the world's information goods and services.[4] I have looked at the list again and have defined it more precisely. Two elements were pertinent in revisiting the 81 corporations: the rapid expansion of data-processing industries* over recent years, which meant the necessary entering of new corporations on the list, and a more exact identification of the corporations' involvement in goods and services in the information sector. In the earlier study corporations were ranked according to their total sales, as has been

---

* This sector will further be referred to as DP industry.

done in most publications. This meant a distortion, since many of them are only partially committed to the information branch of their industrial activities.

The criteria for listing firms as major information corporations have been: their accessibility as public corporations;[5] a sales percentage of information goods and services amounting to at least 10% of their total revenues; a minimum of 10% out of total sales stemming from foreign markets; a volume of information sales that would put them on Fortune's list of 1000 largest industrial corporations; and, leadership in their special sector of the information industry.[6] Meeting these criteria are the 86 transnational corporations ranked according to their information sales in Table 1.

Of the 86 corporations, 40 are 100% involved in the sales of information goods and/or services. For all the corporations the average percentage of information sales as part of total sales is 75%.

The corporations can be divided into three broad categories:

i.   they are *part of industrial conglomerates*-corporations with diversified holdings in a variety of industrial sectors—such as General Electric (i.e., electrical appliances, light bulbs, gas turbines, nuclear reactors, chemicals, and transportation); IT&T (car rentals, frozen food, hotels, insurance); Paramount Pictures (part of Gulf & Western Industries Inc.,: i.e., automobiles, aerospace, minerals, petrochemicals); Warner Communications (part of Kinney Services: i.e., dry cleaners, supermarkets, parking lots); United Artists (part of Transamerica: diversified-financial company);

ii. they are *information conglomerates*-corporations primarily investing in various sectors of the information industry—such as RCA (in telecommunications, broadcasting, records, publishing, and consumer electronics); EMI (in films, records, consumer electronics); MCA (in films, records, publishing); Philips (in DP, telecommunications, records, consumer electronics);

iii. they are primarily *information corporations*-with their chief holding in one sector of the industry—such as IBM (in DP); Burroughs (in DP); Digital Equipment (in DP); AT&T (in telecommunications); Ericsson (in telecommunications); Polygram (in records); the Advertising Agencies and the News Agencies; the Washington Post (in publishing); Sony (in consumer electronics).

The group of 86 corporations can be subdivided in various *sectors* of the information industry.

Sectors are formed by groups of corporations producing/distributing information goods and/or services that can be identified as distinct clusters related to identifiable market segments.

For some groups of corporations there are presently delineated markets where sales and concentration ratios can be calculated, such as the record market, the DP market, or the film market.

The distinctive quality of their product also lumps together such corporations as the newsagencies or the advertising agencies.

Sometimes within broad sectors a more precise division of goods and services can be constructed according to submarkets for categories that within the sector can be lumped together as a distinct group of goods or services.

The division can also be approached from the classical economic distinction between types of goods, such as final consumption goods, intermediate goods or capital goods, and services, such as disseminating or linking services. Linking services are provided by telecommunication network operators, such as COMSAT or AT&T. Disseminating services are provided by, i.a., the advertising agencies or marketing bureaus, or data banks. Final consumption goods are records or TV programs. Intermediate goods stem from data collectors, such corporations being involved in remote resources sensing, or news agencies. Capital goods producers are the mainframe computer manufacturers or firms, such as RCA, building radio/TV stations. Table 2 gives the most important sectors of the information industry with their goods and/or services.

TRANSNATIONALIZATION

An outstanding feature of the development of the information industry is its transnationalization. A process that is intrinsically related to the shift of the world economy over the past decades from local to global markets. The information corporations to transnationalize first were the news agencies, or more precisely their predecessors, such as the German agency Wolff, the French Havas, and the British Reuters that embarked upon their international expansion in the 1870's.[7] At that time the first of a series of "Agency Treaties" was concluded by which the international newsmarket was split up in parts to be allocated as privileged terrain for the leading agencies. Also, the hardware industry was involved early with transnational development. As early as 1883 the Edison Corporation (later AEG) was established in Germany for electrical goods manufacturing in collaboration with the American General Electric Company.[8] Dutch electronics corporation

Philips started its transnational activities in 1893 with exports to Germany and Eastern Europe. Similarly, telecommunications has a long tradition of transnational operations. The first transnational service operations of telephone, telegraphy, and telex of any significance commenced in the 1920s and 1930s. Greater transnational expansion occurred after 1945 and especially beginning in the 1960s with the development of satellite networks. The film industry started its expansion in the 1920s and 1930s. "By the end of this period, American film companies had staked out foreign fields of interest, assumed dominant positions in many markets, and virtually extinguished competition in some others. Management structure for global operation was inaugurated, and the trade organization for Hollywood production and distribution interests created a foreign department to handle the industry's diplomatic work."[9]

Transnational broadcasting originates in the same period with, for example, NBC's radio programs being exported to Latin America in 1927. The TV component comes later and becomes transnationalized from the 1950s.

In general, for all of the information industry sectors, the same observation applies as in the case of advertising. "The foreign expansion of U.S. advertising agencies is intimately linked with the general expansion of U.S. manufacturing, assembling, mining, and agricultural concerns."[10] In their study on transnational advertising Janus and Roncagliolo give the following factors as elementary in the transnationalization process: i) higher growth rates outside the domestic market; ii) higher profit margins outside the domestic market; iii) stimulus by industrial transnational corporations that have entered foreign markets; iv) "pull" from local corporations; and v) the spread of financial risk.

Studying the foreign operations of the 86 information corporations (Table 3) a picture emerges from which the following conclusions can be drawn:

1. The average percentage of foreign sales for the total industry is 36.7%. In the DP sector the foreign percentage is 41%; in the manufacturing of telecommunications equipment it is 44.6%; in advertising 47.7%; in news 35%; and in the film industry 50%. For comparison: in the same year, 1976, the average percentage foreign sales for the 150 largest transnational corporations is 39%. In different industrial sectors the percentages were: for the automotive branch 44.5%, petroleum 37%, and chemical 49%.[11] The information industry is slightly less transnationalized as compared to the industry as a whole. This is due mainly to strong domestic markets

in some of its sectors, such as news. Other sectors though have a significantly strong dependence on foreign markets. Countrywise foreign sales for corporations located in the U.S. average 32.6%, for Westeuropean firms 44.2% and for Japanese corporations 31%.

2. The corporations' headquarters are geographically distributed in the following manner: U.S. 51; U.K. 11; Japan 7; Federal Republic of Germany 6; France 5; Sweden, The Netherlands, Italy, Canada all have 1, there is 1 U.S./U.K. firm and 1 FGR/The Netherlands firm. Almost 60% of the world's largest information transnationals are located in the U.S.

3. The number of foreign subsidiaries for the information industry averages 13.2. Twelve out of the 86 corporations have 25 or more foreign subsidiaries, and the most widespread firm is IBM.

4. Foreign subsidiaries are geographically distributed as follows: In Western Europe: 373, out of which 167 are in four countries; the U.K. (43), The Netherlands (33), France (32), and the Federal Republic of Germany (31).

   In Latin America: 186, out of which 107 are in four countries; Brazil (36), Mexico (31), Argentina (22), and Venezuela (18).

   In Asia 89 out of which 41 are in Japan (16), Hong Kong (15), and Singapore (10).

   In North America: 57, 37 in Canada and 20 in the U.S.

   Australia and New Zealand host 52 foreign subsidiaries.

   Africa has 41 out of which 30 are located in South Africa (18), Nigeria (8) and Kenya (4).

   The conclusion is that of all the foreign subsidiaries that can be identified 54% are located in Western Europe and North America. Latin America, Asia, and Africa have 40%. Fifteen countries (U.S., Canada, U.K., The Netherlands, France, FRG, Japan, Hong Kong, Singapore, South Africa, Nigeria, Kenya, Brazil, Mexico, and Argentina) have 52% of foreign subsidiaries of the leading information transnational corporations.

5. The location of foreign markets is not always clearly indicated in the sources available. Nevertheless, it was possible for a sample of the industry to calculate where foreign revenues stem from. For U.S. corporations:

   • Western Europe 41.9%
   • Canada 13.5%
   • Latin America 5.2%
   • Asia 2.5%

For Westeuropean corporations:

- Other Westeuropean countries 34%
- North America 23%
- Africa 9.2%
- Asia 7%
- Latin America 6.8%
- Australia 6.7%

For both U.S. and Westeuropean corporations, more than 50% of foreign revenues come from markets in Western Europe and North America. Most of the world's information trade takes place between North America and Western Europe.

6. For some sectors in the information industry it is possible to establish specific foreign markets.
   For the largest U.S. advertising agencies (in 1976) foreign sales came from:

- Western Europe: 53.5%
- Latin America: 8.1%
- Canada: 5%
- Australia and New Zealand: 5%
- Asia: 4.2%
- Africa: 2.4% [12]

For computer products the distribution of import markets where important segments of foreign revenues stem from is:

- Western Europe: 55%
- North America: 15.2%
- Latin America: 6.3%
- Asia: 7%
- Africa: 2.5% [13]

For the U.S. film industry there are 75 definable export markets. In 1978 the top five markets were Japan, Canada, France, the United Kingdom, and the Federal Republic of Germany. Over the past 15 years, these markets have accounted for about 44% of export rentals. The top fifteen markets (which additionally include: Italy, Spain, Australia, Mexico, Brazil, The Netherlands, Sweden,

Argentina, South Africa, and Venezuela) have accounted for about 75% of total world rentals.[14]

The market for integrated circuits in 1976 gives the following picture:

- U.S.: 54%
- Japan: 22%
- Western Europe: 20%

For minicomputers the distribution in 1975 is:

- U.S.: 73%
- Western Europe: 18%[15]

THE SECTORS

Data-processing

On the list of the 86 largest information corporations are 24 firms with extensive interests in the data processing industry. As Table 4 indicates, their DP revenues in 1977 amounted to almost $30 billion. Total world DP sales for 1977 could be estimated at some U.S.$40 billion.[16]

In 1979 the global market for DP goods and services surpassed the $50 billion mark.

Subdividing the DP industry, one can distinguish the manufacturers of mainframe computers, minicomputers and peripheral equipment (including terminals), and firms involved in software and service operations. The global market division for 1979 sales was:

- Mainframe computers 16%
- Minicomputers 10%
- Peripheral equipment (incl. terminals) 45%
- Software and services 25%

Tables 5, 6, 7, and 8 show sales for leading firms in sub-sectors of the DP industry.

Telecommunications

The telecommunications field can be subdivided into the manufacturers of telecommunications equipment (such as telephone systems), satellite communications systems (launch vehicles, space vehicles, earth stations), and data communications equipment; telecommunications system operators (such as AT&T, GT&E, IT&T, RCA, and COMSAT with 1976 revenues totalling $35,924 billion), and data communications carriers. For the first two categories, 1976 sales are listed in Tables 9 and 10. Datacom equipment manufacturers and datacom carriers are ranked in Tables 11 and 12.

Other Sectors

For other sectors of the information industry 1976 sales are given in the Tables 13, 14, 15, 16, 17, 18, 19, and 20.

Additionally, the 4 leading international newsagencies show a 1976 total of $296 million.

In assorted information technologies there were over $4.6 billion in sales of photocopying machines and over $1 billion in broadcasting equipment. See Tables 21a and 21b.

In studying sales in the various sectors of the industry, an overview can be constructed of the distribution of total sales as shown in Figure 1. As

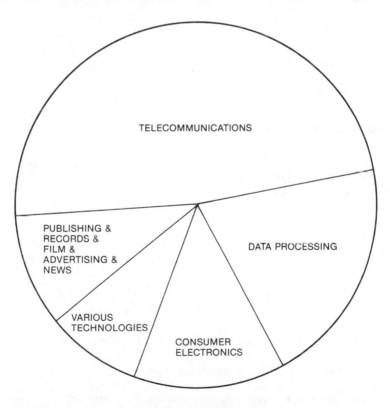

Figure 1 Distribution Sales Information Industry (1976)

can be concluded from this presentation, over 90% of revenues in the industry stem from hardware goods—48% telecommunications, 20% DP, 13.1% consumer electronics; hardly 10% comes from software-type sales, i.e., film sales account for 1.8% and international news for 0.2%.

INTEGRATION OF SECTORS

Many of the corporations in the information industry have activities in more than one sector. The graphic presentation in Figure 2 indicates the density of multi-sector activities. Density was calculated by taking the actual number of sector overlappings, divided by the potential number of overlappings.

Density is an index of "conglomerization" which is apparently very strong in the TV-Film and records business. This is also increasingly important in the DP and telecommunications sectors. Over the past years DP corporations have become involved with telecommunications technology and equipment and vice versa. Examples are IBM in its cooperation with COMSAT and Aetna Life Insurance in Satellite Business Systems, Xerox in its acquisition of Western Union International, one of the largest international record carriers; NCR with investments in equipment in data communications.

Telecommunications corporations have acquired DP firms, such as IT&T buying Booth Courner (dataterminals), GT&E buying Telenet (packet switching), and Northern Telecom buying Danray (Network programming), and Sycor & Data (data terminals). Also the telephone company ("Ma Bell") moved into the data field, AT&T developed intelligent terminals and designed networks for data transmission.[17] The DP-telecommunications convergence is also shown in Tables 11 and 12. DP firms are manufacturing datacom equipment, and traditional record carriers are among the leading datacom carriers.

There is also a tendency for overlapping between the DP firms and the electronic components manufacturers, cf., Philips, RCA, and Texas Instruments.

This is symptomatic for the trend towards vertical integration, which is characteristic for the information industry. It can also be observed in cases where publishing companies get involved with their raw material, paper and wood products (cf., Time Inc. and the New York Times Co.).

THE COMPLEX

'The fundamental presumption of a largely free market economy, as in the United States, is that whenever possible there should be maximum

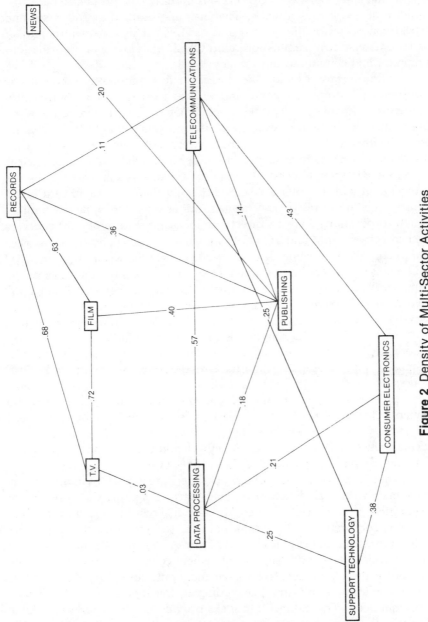

Figure 2 Density of Multi-Sector Activities

competition among private sector organizations for the production and distribution of goods and services. This also applies to the production and distribution of information goods and services." This statement is part of the U.S. Government submission to an OECD conference on information, computer, and communications policy.[18]

On the surface it looks indeed as if the international production and distribution of information goods and services is carried out in a sufficiently competitive climate by at least 86 contending parties with diverse interests. Closer analysis, however, reveals that the information industry is characterized by its complex nature, i.e., the intricate web of its interlocks. The information industry is interwoven with other industrial interests (as is clear in the case of the conglomerates), with financial interests (as we shall discuss further), and with the military.[19] Additionally there is a significant intra-industry network of relations. This has various dimensions. Between information corporations there are direct interlocks in the form of *joint ventures* (such as between IBM and COMSAT in Satellite Business Systems, between Philips and MCA in the production of video-discs, between MCA and IBM in Discovision Associates, between TRW and Fujitsu for the sales of DP equipment); *joint ownership* of subsidiaries (such as between Philips and Siemens with Polygram, between NCR, Control Data, and ICL with CPI, between Honeywell and Control Data with MPI); *stockholdings* (such as in the case of Kirk Kerkorian holding significant volumes of voting stock in both MGM and Columbia Pictures, GE holding 11% of the stock in Toshiba, Philips holding 24.5% of the Grundig stock, Saint Gobain-Pont-à-Mousson holding 10% in CII Honeywell-Bull and 33⅓% in Olivetti), *licensing, supply, sales, or production agreements* (such as between Fujitsu and Siemens, Honeywell and Nippon Electric, Xerox and Mitsubishi, Olivetti and Hitachi, AEG/Telefunken and Thomson/Brandt), *joint directorates* (such as between IBM and Time, Honeywell and GE, Interpublic and CBS, McGraw Hill and Sperry Rand, ICL and Plessey).

In addition to these direct interlocks there are important indirect interlocks, mainly through directorates. Such interlocks imply that directors of corporation A meet directors of corporation B across the boardroom tables of X other corporations. This means that what seem to be major competitors in the information industry such as IBM and AT&T have 22 indirect routes through which they could "supply convenient conduits for possible private solution of the public debate between monopoly and competition in the telecommunications industry", according to the report of a U.S. Senate Subcommittee.[20] The indirect interlocks provide, as the report comments, "substantial opportunity for direct policy discussions and potential understandings among these major competitors."[21] Such discussion and understanding is very likely to reduce genuine competition to what has become to be termed as "courteous competition."

In Figure 3 the network of direct and indirect interlocks between Westeuropean, Japanese, and U.S. participants in the information industry are shown. Additionally the links between those U.S. corporations interlocked with the Westeuropeans and the Japanese are shown in Figure 4.

Strong direct interlocks characterize the film industry particularly as Figure 5 indicates. The large U.S. broadcasting networks have significant indirect interlocks and are linked to the leading firm in the information business, IBM (Figure 6).

For the 25 U.S. information corporations that are most strongly interlocked the network is shown in Figure 7.

The corporations with most intra-industry interlocks (both direct and indirect) are:

Corporation	Direct Interlocks	Indirect Interlocks
IBM	6	120
AT&T	3	117
GE	4	83
Time	3	55
Xerox	1	50
RCA	2	47
Sperry	2	47
CBS	1	42

The total number of direct interlocks between information corporations is 119, out of which 64 are between U.S. firms, 47 between Westeuropean firms, and 8 between Japanese firms.

In terms of geographical distribution most corporations interlock with corporations located in the same region. For North American firms:

- 84% of the interlocks are with North American firms;
- 12% of the interlocks are with Westeuropean firms, and
- 4% of the interlocks are with Japanese firms

For Westeuropean firms:

- 79% of the interlocks are with Westeuropean firms;
- 17% of the interlocks are with North American firms, and
- 4% of the interlocks are with Japanese firms

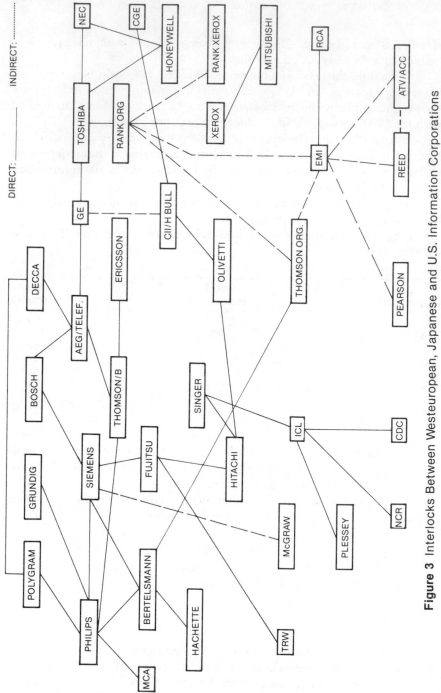

Figure 3 Interlocks Between Westeuropean, Japanese and U.S. Information Corporations

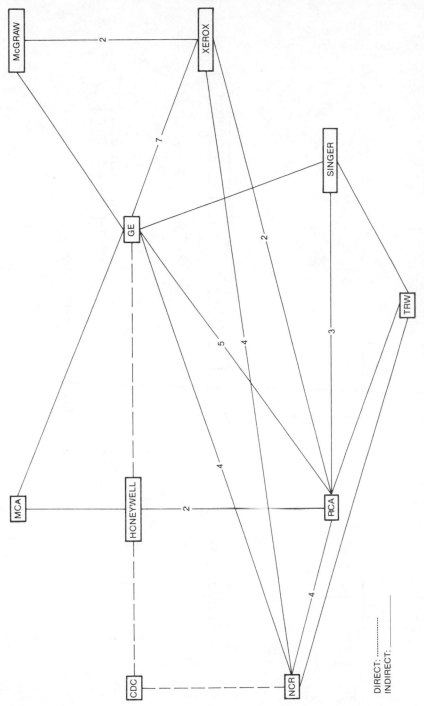

Figure 4 Interlocks Between U.S. Corporations Interlocked with Westeuropean and Japanese Companies

DIRECT: ……………
INDIRECT: ————

27

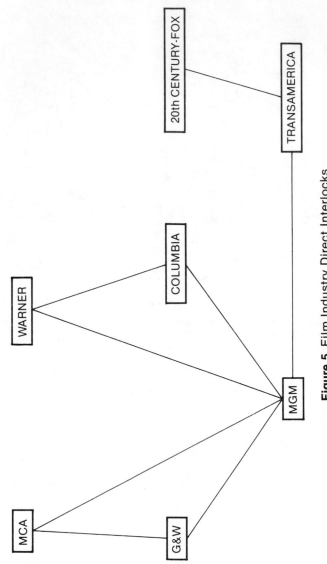

Figure 5 Film Industry Direct Interlocks

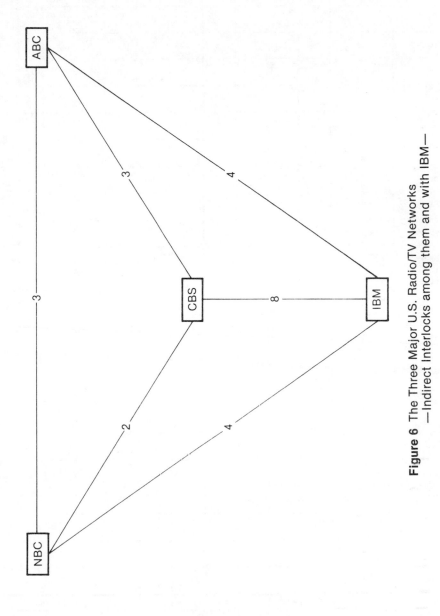

Figure 6 The Three Major U.S. Radio/TV Networks
—Indirect Interlocks among them and with IBM—

	IBM	AT&T	GE	Time	Xerox	RCA	Sperry	CBS	Rock-well	Lock-heed	COM-SAT	NCR
IBM		22	13	15 \ 1	10	4	5	8	3	6	3 \ 1	5
AT&T	22		14	3 \ 1	12	3	7	6	6	6	5	2
GE	13	14		3 \ 1	7	5	9	3	3	4	4	4
Time	15 \ 1	3 \ 1	3 \ 1		4	3		5	3	2	2	2
Xerox	10	12	7	4		2	1	1	1			4
RCA	4	3	5	3	2		2	2	1	2	2	4
Sperry	5	7	9		1	2		3	1		4	2
CBS	8	6	3	5	1	2	3		2	1		2
Rockwell	3	6	3	3	1	1	1	2		3	2	
Lockheed	6	6	4	2		2		1	3		3	
COMSAT	3 \ 1	5	4	2		2	4		2	3		2
NCR	5	2	4	2	4	4	2	2			2	
ABC	4	2	2		1	3	4	3				2
IT&T	3	4	1		1	1	2	2	3	3		1
Honeywell	2	4	1 \ 1	2		2	2	1		1		
Singer	3	2	1	3		3	1				3	
N.Y. Times	3 \ 2	3	4	1	2							1
TRW	2	3		2		1	1		1	1	4	1
GT&E	2	2		1	2	3				1		
McG. Hill	1	1 \ 1	1	1	2		1 \ 1		1			
Interpublic	2	1				1		1 \ 1	2	1		
Disney		1		1		1			1	2	1	1
MCA	1	1		1						2		
W. Post	1 \ 1	2	1	1					1			1
LTV	1	2	1				2					

ABC	IT&T	Honey-well	Singer	N.Y. Times	TRW	GT&E	McG. Hill	Inter-public	Disney	MCA	W. Post	LTV
4	3	2	3	3 / 2	2	2	1	2		1	1 / 1	1
2	4	4	2	3	3	2	1 / 1	1	1	1		2
2	1	1 / 1	1	4			1					1
	2		3	1	2	1	1		1	1	1	
1	1			2		2	2					
3	1	2	3		1	3		1	1			
4	2	2	1		1		1 / 1					2
3	2	1					1 / 1	1			1	
	3				1	1	1 / 1	2	2	2		
	3	1			1			1	1			
			3		4				1			
2	1			1	1						1	
	1		1		1							1
1								1				
									1	1		
1					1							
						2					1 / 1	
1			1									
				2								
	1								1			
		1						1				
		1										
				1 / 1								
1												

One figure = indirect interlocks
Right upper = direct interlocks
Left below = indirect interlocks

31

For Japanese firms:

- 50% of the interlocks are with Japanese firms;
- 25% of the interlocks are with North American firms, and
- 25% of the interlocks are with Westeuropean firms

In terms of competition on specific sectorial markets it is also pertinent to look at interlocks between corporations within an industry sector. For 7 sectors the comparative density of interlocks was calculated by taking the actual number of interlocks divided by the potential number of interlocks.

Sector	Density of Interlocks
Data-processing	0.08
Telecommunications equipment	0.16
TV film production	0.20
Theatrical film production	0.17
Publishing	0.13
Records	0.11
Consumer electronics	0.09

A comparison of interlocks between selected industry sectors gives the following picture:

Sectors	Number of Interlocks Between 10 Largest Corporations in Each Sector
DP & Telecommunications	77
DP & Consumer electronics	50
DP & Theatrical film production	5
Telecommunications & Consumer electronics	48
Records & publishing	21

A particular connection to analyze in the information industry is the combined interest in hardware and software sectors. The industry counts a number of corporations that are active in both areas. They are: the U.S. firms—RCA, Xerox, IT&T, Litton, Singer, Lockheed; the U.K. firms—EMI, Rank, Decca; the German firm, Siemens, and the Dutch firm, Philips.

There are direct and indirect interlocks between leading firms in hardware sectors and dito firms in software sectors. Significant are: *IBM*, interlocks with Time, CBS, ABC, New York Times, McGraw Hill, Washington Post, Interpublic, and MCA; *General Electric*, interlocks with Time, CBS, ABC, New York Times, and McGraw Hill; *RCA*, interlocks with CBS,

ABC, Time, Interpublic, and Disney Productions; *EMI,* interlocks with Thomson, Pearson, Reed, and ATV/ACC; *Philips,* interlocks with MCA, Polygram; *Siemens* interlocks with Polygram, and Bertelsmann.

These 6 firms also have several interlocks among themselves

- IBM and GE count 13 indirect interlocking directorates;
- RCA has 4 interlocks with IBM and 5 with GE;
- RCA and EMI are interlocked;
- Philips and Siemens are interlocked

In addition to their hardware-software connections and interlocks, the 6 firms are leaders in some market sectors and have important interests in others.

IBM leads in the DP industry with a market segment of over 50%. GE leads in satellite manufacturing with 26% of the market and has 4% of consumer electronics. Philips and Siemens combine through Polygram in the records industry with 16.5% of the market. Philips has 19% of consumer electronics, and 3% in telecommunications equipment. Siemens has 8% in telecommunications equipment and 2% in DP. RCA has 5% of satellite manufacturing, 11.5% in records, 6% in publishing, and 4.5% in consumer electronics. EMI has 9% in the film industry and 17% in records.

If one combines the interests of these 6 firms they account for:

- 53% of the DP market,
- 11% of the telecommunications equipment market,
- 31% of the satellite equipment market,
- 45% of the records market, and
- 27.5% of the consumer electronics market

The 6 account for 23% of total information industry sales. They account for 21% of all direct intra-industry interlocks.

OLIGOPOLIZATION

"Ever since advertising expenditures exploded three years ago, Madison Avenue has looked like Merger Street" wrote P. W. Bernstein in *Fortune* of August 1979. "The wave of mergers and acquisitions among ad agencies has given a new image to the industry of image makers."[22]

In November 1978 Interpublic, the holding company that already owned McCann Erickson, Campbell-Ewald, and Marschalk & Erwin Wasey, announced the acquisition of SSC&B. In June 1979 Young & Rubicam announced the acquisition of the 20th largest U.S. advertising agency, Marsteller. Other large agencies were studying new acquisitions.

Merging is like interlocking, yet another factor to distort the operation of the free market system; it creates large corporations in certain sectors with increasing control of market segments. This trend towards oligopolized markets is very strong in the information industry. The implication is that there is little or no place for small or medium-sized firms. A key requirement for the existence of a free, competitive market—the possibility for new firms to enter—is therefore not met. Oligopolized markets in certain sectors also provide a few corporations with the capacity to expand in other sectors.

Oligopolization has existed in most information industry sectors for some time. Between the two world wars international advertising was already largely in the hands of two agencies: J. Walter Thompson and McCann. The film industry has had a strong degree of concentration since the 1920's, when 8 major companies practically controlled production, distribution, and exhibition (Paramount, Warner Bros., 20th Century Fox, Loew's Inc., United Artists, Universal Pictures, RKO, and Columbia).[23] From the outset the development of the film industry has been determined by a tendency towards decisive influence upon the market for maintaining and expanding profits.[24] "This oligopolistic structure not only controlled the U.S. industry, it also already dominated the world industry and drew a significant proportion of its revenues and profits from the non-U.S. market."[25]

For the record industry Chapple and Garofalo give the following account: "The industry did not begin with a number of small companies gradually becoming to be monopolized by a few powerful firms. From the beginning a few, two or three, large firms have accounted for a majority of industry volume. The major reason for this is that the two biggest record companies have since 1900 been linked to phonograph firms and since the thirties to large broadcasting and electronics corporations."[26]

The international production and distribution of news has been dominated by four large agencies since late in the 19th century.

The beginning of concentration in the data processing sector is of more recent date. In the early 1950's the U.S. industry supplied more than 95% of the world market. Among these U.S. firms one company had the uncontested leader position: IBM. During the sixties its market share was estimed to vary between 66 and 72%.[27]

Since their origins not much has changed in the various industry sectors as the following paragraphs will indicate.

DP Industry

"The international computer market is still dominated by the products of American firms, manufactured either in the United States or by these firms' foreign subsidiaries."[28] In 1975 these firms supplied 87% of the world market. In the same year IBM had a turnover amounting to 63.3% of total DP industry sales and had 85.5% share of world profits. In 1977 sales out of the 24 largest transnational DP firms IBM obtained almost 50%.

For many years now DP products' prices and DP technology development have been defined by IBM control of the industry, leaving little room for other contenders and hardly any room for new entrants. The strength of IBM has made it possible for this firm to become vertically integrated in a strict sense, i.e.,, manufacturing the whole range of products within the DP range. IBM now produces, alongside its large general purpose computers, the small business systems machines. It also manufactures its own components and through this achieves an easy access into the microprocessor market.

On the somewhat less concentrated minicomputer market, in 1976 the largest firm, Digital Equipment Corporation, had a marketshare of 34.6%. The four largest corporations controlled together 64.7%.

Film Industry

"The battle between the Anti-Trust division of the Justice Department and the U.S. majors is a long saga beginning with the first case against Paramount in 1922 and continuing at present with action, for example, to restrain Kerkorian of MGM gaining control of Columbia."[29]

As Garnham comments the tendency towards oligopoly "is exaggerated in the movie business because of its specific characteristics."[30] In this sector the factor distribution is of crucial importance. To achieve a profitable balance between the large investments in production and the revenues from cinemas, the control of distribution networks is essential. This enables access to the world market, which for many years accounted for some 50% of U.S. film industry rentals. "The maintenance of a world-wide distribution network is expensive (approximately 20 million dollars per year currently), thus barriers to entry are very high."[31] On the domestic market 6 U.S. film companies had almost 89.1% of movie distribution in 1978.

Corporation	Share U.S. Movie Distribution[32]
Paramount	23.8%
Universal	16.8%
20th Century Fox	13.4%
Warner Bros.	13.2%
Columbia	11.6%
United Artists	10.3%

Out of an estimated 1976 world market of 2.5 billion dollars the 10 largest firms account for 66%.[33]

Record Industry

The strongly oligopolized record industry has, nevertheless, throughout its history seen the existence of small independent labels, especially
facilitated by technological developments that made phonograph production relatively cheap. The small firms' product, however, remained limited
to highly specialized and/or local markets. As with the film industry the
key factor is distribution, in particular, for international production.
Again, reliance on international large scale distribution networks makes the
industry economically viable for the large corporations only. Corporations
such as RCA, which since 1970 also distributes the records produced by
20th Century Fox, or MCA, also distributing for ABC records, or EMI/
Capitol, distributing for United Artists.

The record industry has seen a phenomenal growth over the past 15
years with its volume increasing fivefold between 1964 and 1978.[34] For 1978
the world market can be estimated at over 10 billion dollars.

The U.S. market comprises 4.2 billion dollars (in retail sales) and is
85% controlled by CBS, Capitol (subsidiary of EMI), RCA, Polygram, and
Warner Communications. Market leader is the German-Dutch combination
Polygram with sales exceeding 1.6 billion dollars.[35] In 1977 the record world
market was almost 8 billion dollars.[36] Some 60% was in the hands of CBS,
EMI, Polygram, Warner Communications, and RCA. (See Table 22.)

The large record companies are integrated in the largest manufacturers
of consumer electronics, such as Philips, Siemens, or EMI; or they are part
of leading information conglomerates, such as CBS, RCA, ABC, or Warner.

Advertising

"The growth of the transnational agencies since 1960 has been truly
phenomenal."[37] This is expected to continue into the 1980s, until worldwide
advertising will be practically controlled by some 10 to 15 large firms.[38]

Worldwide revenues in 1979 for the 50 largest advertising agencies was
3.9 billion dollars. The ten largest U.S. agencies garnered some 46% of this.

Electronic Components Industry

In the manufacturing of discrete components, such as diodes and tran-
sistors, the world market is virtually controlled by three firms, Texas Instruments, Motorola, and Fairchild. In the integrated circuits manufacturing the
same firms play a considerable role, but there are more contenders as Table
19 shows.

Out of an estimated world volume of semiconductor sales of slightly
over 3 billion dollars (1975), Texas Instruments, Philips, and Motorola controlled 43%. (See Table 23.)

In the period 1974–1976 the market for microprocessors was strongly dominated (over 75%) by Intel, Rockwell, Texas Instruments, and Motorola.

Paper Industry

"In the capitalist producing countries the paper industry is in the hands of a very small number of companies."[39]

The most important producers are headquartered in the U.S., with a leading position for International Paper—the price regulator for the world paper market. Other information industries heavily involved in paper production include the *New York Times, Washington Post, Time,* IT&T and Reed International. "The concentration of paper concerns is favored by the concentration of global paper production in a small number of industrial regions. Approximately 80% of world paper production originates from the U.S., Japan, Canada, Scandinavia, the USSR and the FRG. A few turnover billionaires in the paper industry of the western nations have the ability to regulate the global market."[40]

CONCENTRATION RATIOS

In measuring degrees of concentration in the sectors of the information industry, the classical indication of the market share of the largest traders in a sector is used. In the present survey the sales mentioned are not fully identical with total world sales in the various sectors, but from different sources it can be determined that the "86" account for some 75% of global sales in information goods and services. The ten largest firms in most of the sectors account for an average of 66% of the world sales in their sector. In the literature one finds different ways of determining the concentration ratio. In the present study the sales of the three largest firms in a sector were taken as a percentage of the sales of the ten largest firms of the world.[41] A strong oligopolistic market can be said to exist in cases where the three firms have over 50% of the sales and a somewhat less oligopolistic market is indicated where there is a share of between 33% and 50% by the three largest. Table 24 gives the overview.

INFORMATION INDUSTRY IS BIG BUSINESS

Conglomerization, integration, interlocking and concentration all point to the conclusion that the transnational information-industrial complex knows no free market or open competition. This is very large business for very large corporations only.

This conclusion invites some further analysis of the economic scope of the information industry.

The information industry includes 8 corporations with sales exceeding 4 billion dollars, 27 corporations with sales between 1 and 4 billion dollars, and 18 corporations with sales between 500 million and 1 billion dollars. The combined 1976 sales of the information industrials reached 147 billion dollars.

There is no doubt in U.S. business and government circles that the information industry and its various sectors have to be considered as vital to the U.S. and the world economy. As the President of Arthur D. Little, John F. Magee testified in a session of a U.S. Senate Subcommittee, "In our information-orientated world communications is a key building block in creating a sound infrastructure for economic growth."[42]

The National Association of Manufacturers stated in a letter to the chairman of the U.S. House Subcommittee on Government Information and Individual Rights, "The indications are that the information technology sector will be critical for the United States as it faces the intensely competitive world economic situation for the 80's. Our world leadership in this field will benefit American trade directly, through the export of goods and services in this sector itself, and indirectly through improving the competitive efficiency of U.S. companies world-wide in all sectors."[43]

At the March 1980 hearings of the same U.S. Subcommittee, Assistant Secretary of Commerce, Harry Geller, stressed the vital importance of U.S. exports in telecommunications and other information goods. "Telecommunications and information merchandise exports represented 10% of the overall U.S. merchandise exports in 1977. Overall, the telecommunications and information sector, together with agriculture and aviation, are currently the leading portions of the export market for the United States."[44] For the U.S. film industry the Film Council declared already in 1936, "Today the movie world is one of major industries of the country," and at its 50th anniversary, the advertising trade journal, *Advertising Age,* described advertising as "the brick and mortar of the U.S. economy."[45]

On a *Fortune* list of the 50 leading U.S. exporters of 1979 there are 10 firms connected with the information industry, seven of them belong to the "86," see Table 25. The information corporations account for 25% of the export sales of the 50.

The information industry is very strongly a growth industry as is clear from developments in its various sectors.

In the DP industry, sales of computers, peripherals, and services are growing at 17% annually. A significant proportion of the DP market is in

Western Europe (some 26%) where for the period 1980–1985 a fivefold increase of the DP market is expected.[46]

On the U.S. market for mini- and microcomputers the rate of growth from 1978 to 1979 was approximately 23% and was predicted to be 35% in 1980. Worldwide DP trade increased between 1975 and 1979 more than twofold. From 1977–1979 the 5 largest DP firms in the world increased their revenues with an average of 31%. In 1980 the DP market in the U.S. grew with approximately 20% and was expected to grow another 26.2% in 1981. In 1980 U.S. exports of DP equipment increased 36.4% over 1979.[47]

In telecommunications equipment the annual market growth is 8%. In the EEC countries, accounting for 29% of telecommunications equipment purchases, an annual growth rate of 6.9% is expected up to 1986, which would bring the European market to reach 13.2 billion dollars.[48]

In the electronic components industry the expectation is a doubling of world-wide sales for integrated circuits in the period up to 1985.

Rapid growth also shows up in the advertising sector, due to the fact that in most of the industrialized countries expenses for advertising have been rising since 1976 and increasingly exceed the growth of gross domestic products. World-wide spending for advertising was 70 billion dollars in 1977, and in 1979 it reached 96.8 billion dollars.[49] Some observers expect a growth up to 125 billion dollars by 1985.[50]

CAPITAL INTENSIVE

Advertising is not only an information industry sector, it also represents a major expenditure in the industry itself. This is not surprising since highly oligopolistic markets demand extensive advertising out of necessity. Looking at the 100 leading U.S. advertisers in 1979, one finds among them 12 firms involved in the information industry, as compared to eight in 1976. Together they spent 1.4 billion dollars in 1979 for the advertising of their products and services. (See Table 26.) Also, there are information corporations among non-U.S. advertisers in leading positions. In 1978 Philips was the largest spender on advertising in the Netherlands with Dfl. 17.7 million. Bosch was No. 11 in the FRG in 1978 with DM43 million. In France, Thomson-Brandt was the third largest advertiser with FF 70.2 million, and Hachette was No. 25 with FF 32 million. In 1977 Reed International was Britain's eighth largest advertiser with £9.8 million.

Product promotion is a major expenditure in the record industry, where promotion budgets for top selling categories such as rock music have increased three times over the past five years.

"Promotion is 70 percent of the record business" says Harry Anger, senior vice president for marketing with Polygram.[51] Fees can also be very high in other sectors of the industry, as Barbara Walter's one million dollars per year contract with ABC TV News showed. In this respect the annual salaries of senior executives in the information corporations make interesting reading. (See Table 27.)

Another aspect of capital intensity in the record industry is the rapidly increasing front investment which, for example, in a rock music LP album has risen from $100.000 to $250.000 during the past five years.[52] This is caused by the costs of sophisticated recording equipment and the high royalties for musicians and fees for producers. MCA, for example, paid Elton John $8 million for a five year contract in the mid-Seventies. Warner Brothers guaranteed Paul Simon $13 million in 1978 for his transfer from CBS. CBS is reported as having signed an $8 million contract with Paul McCartney in 1979 for three albums.

Capital investment for production is also on the increase in the film sector. In 1969 the U.S. film companies released four pictures costing over $10 million, ten years later eight productions were exceeding the $15 million mark. Trade journal, *Variety*, comments on this development: "After nearly a decade of budgets being kept relatively in line, costs are now running apace with increase in the overall market and companies, buoyed by the runaway success of their top grossers, are tending to spend as if recent high earnings represented the norm." The journal adds to this: "with budgets now hitting such highs with increasing regularity, the margin for error will quickly narrow and once two or three of the current crop of massively budgeted pictures flop, companies may well take a hard look at the kind of financial commitments they are currently making on a repeated basis."[53] Table 28 gives an extract of information from *Variety* on some recent high budgeted pictures.

The increasing costs of production are due to the considerable expansion of fixed capital in the industry, i.e., capital to be invested in the means of production, such as studios, technical equipment, special effects. According to F. E. Rosenfelt (chairman of MGM) the break-even point of the average motion-picture reaches $16 million. The average production cost in 1980 has risen to $10 million and the marketing cost to $6 million.[54] To a certain extent this increase of fixed capital is matched with the expansion of variable capital due to rising costs for honoraria of the labor involved. The labor component in the film industry is very capital intensive. As mentioned before, distribution is possible only through very expensive international networks, and also exhibition has become more capital intensive with the emergence of luxurious cinemas.

The larger the volume of fixed capital, the larger the risks for capital to be invested in film production. This, in turn, leads to greater control by financiers and less likelihood for small, independent producers to get credit.

Another sector of the information industry, telecommunications, has exchanged its labor intensity for capital intensity. This sector used to employ large volumes of factory workers, maintenance crews, and systems operators. Increasingly new technologies make them redundant. Electronic exchanges in the telephone system, for example, can be manufactured, maintained, and operated by a few people with specialized computer technique skills. Between 1974 and 1977 large telecommunications equipment manufacturers, such as Philips, Siemens, and Western Electric reduced employment with 5 to 25%.

A crucial factor in the increasing capital needs in this sector are the costs of research and development, similar to those in the DP industry and the electronic components industry. High expenditures are made for the exploration and implementation of such techniques as optical fibers, lasers, and microprocessors.

In 1977, the combined average percentage of sales spent on R&D for U.S. aerospace, dataprocessing, and electronics was 4.1%, as compared to 2.5% in another R&D intensive industry, the chemical industry. In 1979 R&D expenditures in the U.S. DP industry were considerably greater than in all manufacturing.[55]

In the Federal Republic of Germany, the electrical/electronics industry spent 6.4% of sales on R&D in 1978, which compares with 4.7% in chemicals, 5.7% in automotive, and 3% in engineering and mining. Some of the leading FRG firms spent more, like Siemens with 10% and AEG/Telefunken with 7% of total turnovers. A survey of R&D percentages spent by selected firms in dataprocessing is given in Table 29.

On a global scale, it can be estimated that R&D expenditure for information technology amounts to some 30% of the world research and development budget.[56]

This demands large funds and attracts large investments, both from private and governmental sources. Among large investors there is increasing interest in corporations' R&D figures.[57]

In the information industry the more traditional mass media sectors are also capital intensive and in need of increasing investments for their fixed costs. Large fixed capital is needed in the publishing industry, i.a., for the costs of paper and printing ink. Over the last decade, prices for the paper used for most magazines have doubled and printing inks have, over the past five years, increased by some 40%. Some cannot comply with this demand and are forced out of the business. During 1980 there were two illustrative examples. The U.S. international newsagency, UPI, made increasing losses (up to some $7 million) and its owner E. W. Scripps Co. was forced to seek a buyer, as were the U.K. papers *The Times* and *The Sunday Times* that confronted the Thomson Organization with considerable losses.

Throughout the historical development of the mass media there is a series of different stages corresponding with particular forms of financing. Roughly one can distinguish four stages.

STAGE I

This is the period in which the first small scale media industries (printed press) find their origin. Production, distribution, and financing are strongly integrated. Ownership and management are combined in the person of the private entrepreneur (financer, banker, or merchant) who founds and finances the medium. Examples can be found in the European newspapers of the 18th and 19th century, such as *The Times*, which was established by its owner, manager, and editor, John Walter.

STAGE II

In this period there is a development towards differentiation in the processes of production, distribution, and financing. With the emerging media of nationwide mass circulation, the need for outside financing grows and creates the separation of management and financing. Different sources of outside financing without immediate involvement in the production are: government subsidies and advertising (example: the newspapers in Europe), banks (example: the film industry in the U.S. from 1920), groups of private persons (example: the case of *Le Monde:* The Beuve-Méry group and their initial capital of 200.000 francs), and the dispersion of stock among large segments of the general public (especially in the U.S. since 1930).

STAGE III

The period of further expansion (mainly nationally) of the media industries and the growing need for large volumes of capital. This has been especially true since 1945, with the trend towards concentration in the media through horizontal and vertical integration and, most importantly, through diversification. Financing is increasingly possible with large corporations' own internal funds.

STAGE IV

This is the period in which transnationalization of the information industry occurs, especially since the 1960s. This takes place concurrently with the transnationalization of banking and the general trend towards concentration of industrial ownership. Industrial ownership shifts from individual stockholders to corporate ownership by financial institutions and other industrial corporations. The significance of outside institutional investors for the financing of the media increases.

Debts

The need for large capital investment raises the question of the indebtedness of corporations in the information industry.

For 55 corporations it was possible to establish their long-term debt/ assets ratio as an indicator of their position as light to heavy borrowers of funds. Table 30 gives the data. Nineteen corporations are moderate to heavy borrowers. The six heavy borrowers are AT&T, GT&E, Control Data, Northern Telecom, LTV, and MGM.

Profits

The capacity to attract large investors' funds will evidently be determined to a large extent by the profitability of the industrial sector. However, in the case of the media there is the additional dimension of potential influence of a political-ideological nature and, for example, the prestigous glamour of controlling a respectable newspaper.[58]

For 57 corporations, indicators of profitability in the form of the rate of return on revenues could be calculated. (See Appendix I)

In 1976: the profit ratio of the 500 largest U.S. corporations was 4.6%
the profit ratio of the U.S. information corporations was 6.0%
the profit ratio of the 500 largest non-U.S. corporations was 4.2%
the profit ratio of the non-U.S. information corporations was 3.4%
In 1979: the profit ratio of the 500 largest U.S. corporations was 5.2%
the profit ratio of the U.S. information corporations was 6.8%
the profit ratio of the 500 largest non-U.S. corporations was 3.2%
the profit ratio of the non-U.S. information corporations was 3.4%
the profit ratio for Westeuropean information corporations was 3.5%
the profit ratio for Japanese information corporations was 3.0%.

An overall comparison for 1979 indicates for the information industry a 5.1% profit ratio as compared to 4.2% for the 1000 largest industrials in the world.

INFORMATION INDUSTRY AND FINANCE

Information corporations are, however, not only borrowers of money, several of them are also lending to finance their own and others' operations. This happens also in other industries. Ford Motors, for example, owns Ford Motor Credit Co., for the financing of Ford cars. This credit company passed the $1 billion mark in non-auto credits in 1979, which, in fact, makes Ford owner of a small bank. As *Forbes* magazine describes such "pushy captive finance companies": "They raised money largely on the reputation of the parent, and used the funds to finance sales of the parent's products. But they have accumulated such financial power over the years that now they can, and do, compete powerfully with the banks and contribute substantially to the parent's earnings."[59]

Table 31 lists finance companies and their income for some corporations in the information industry. Five of them belong to the ten largest finance companies in the U.S. in 1977 (Table 32).

Finance is also important to the information industry in the form of "financial information." Some information corporations have specialized financial information services or media. Examples are S. Pearson, which owns the *Financial Times*; TRW Inc., with its Information Services Division for consumer and business credit reporting and TRW Business Credit for credit reporting to the business community; and McGraw Hill, with financial information services through Standard & Poor's Co. and S&P Compustat Services Inc. with credit data for major banks.

Most important are financial information services in the news sector. All the major news agencies have such services. Since 1968 the French agency AFP operates SET (economic information service with telex connections). By the end of the 1970s, SET had some 104 subscribers, a majority of which belonged to the French business and banking community. The U.S. agency A.P. links up with the Dow Jones News Agency, and this combination started its Telerate Systems service in the late 1970s to counter Reuters' leadership on the financial data market. The other U.S. agency, UPI, operates, since 1977, with the Knight-Ridders newspaper group the Commodity News Service. Also UPI sells its financial news to Alpex Computer Corp. for electronic publishing. Most elaborately involved in financial information services is the British agency Reuters. This involvement has transformed the agency from primarily a general news distributor to the "electronic floor" of the international money market. The general news coverage for newspapers, radio, and TV stations accounted for some 75–80% of Reuters' total revenues (£3 million) in 1963. In 1976 these services had a significantly lower contribution to the total turnover: some 18% of the total £41 million.[60] In 1980 out of a total £80 million revenues 15% came from the mass media.[61]

Reuters economic services consist of quotations, news and background information for three main areas of business: Money, Investment and Commodities. This information is disseminated in a variety of ways from computerized retrieval quotations devices to hard copy teleprinter display and printed bulletins. Services are provided on an international and national basis.

The teleprinter services such as the Reuter Money Report provide bankers, governments, industrialists and traders with an authoritative source of world money news. The Reuter Monitor is a computerized video interrogation service designed for the real time distribution of money rates and news throughout the world. The rates on the service are directly contributed by leading international banks and financial institutions.

The teleprinter services, such as the Reuter Financial Report and the Reuter Securities Report, cover company news and stock market prices from all the major world exchanges. The Reuter-Ultronic Videomaster and Stockmaster are desk-top interrogation devices enabling subscribers to retrieve quotations and related information on domestic and international stock markets. The Reuter Monitor Securities service provides instantaneous access to stock and related information quoted directly by brokers, banks and other institutions. Custom price is a service of raw data consisting of upwards of 27,000 daily stock prices and is supplied on punched cards, magnetic tape, disc or in print-out form.

The teleprinter services about commodities consist of prices and reports from the leading world markets on a wide range of commodities, including metals, cocoa, sugar, coffee, grains, edible oils and oilseeds, rubber, wool and shipping. The Reuter-Ultronic Videomaster and Stockmaster also provide prices from the world's commodity markets.[62]

In February 1981 Reuters launched a computerized money dealing system which had taken 5 years and £8 million to develop. Its services are available to the U.S., Canada and seven Westeuropean countries and allow banks in these countries to deal instantaneously on the money market from terminals on which the latest money rates in each country are shown. The system is expected to improve the speed of interbank dealing and at its start 160 banks had subscribed for £1.500 each per month.[63]

The news media have always had an important function as channels for financial and economic news. Various studies on the content of international news flow make it possible to estimate that such news occupies between 6%

and 20% of the total news coverage.[61] It also has to be noted that many of the European newspapers started in fact as financial news pamphlets, such as the predecessor of *Le Monde, Le Temps*, with information on the French stock market, or the predecessor of the *Frankfurter Allgemeine Zeiting* (the *Frankfurter Handelszeitung*) with stock exchange information and more general economic news. Also, the *British Times* started primarily as medium for market news. At the end of last century there was a lively bribing of newspapers in France with the purpose of promoting the sales of certain stock. One finds among the first and most important clientele of European newspapers and news agencies the representatives of the business community, especially the banks.[65]

Nowadays an extra impetus to move into financial information services is the saturation of the market for general news and the necessity to explore new and cheaper communication channels. Growing costs of telephone lines, for example, have led to the exploitation of new techniques, such as satellite transmissions.[66]

SUMMARY

The main characteristics of the transnational information industry are:

- The industry is largely controlled by a network of 86 corporations with an average 75% involvement in the production/distribution of information goods and services. The network is strongly interlocked. Corporations tend to interlock with corporations in the same geographical region. The strongest interlocks are found between the DP sector and the Telecommunications sector.
- The industry is very capital intensive.
- 60% of the corporations in the industry are headquartered in the USA. 54% of foreign subsidiaries are located in North America and Western Europe.
- Most of the trade in information goods and services is between North America and Western Europe.
- The markets in the different sectors of the industry show a strong degree of oligopolization. This is particularly so in the DP sector and the Telecommunications sector.
- Goods and services in the DP and Telecommunications sectors account for 68% of total industry sales.

In order to identify the group of corporations that constitute the nucleus of the complex, the 86 corporations were measured against the following criteria:

- transnationalization (over 50% foreign revenues);
- profitability (over 6% profit ratio);
- industry interlocks, especially hardware-software connections;
- market position (among the leading corporations in a sector);
- diversification in different information industry sectors (three or more).

Meeting at least three of these criteria are the following eight corporations: IBM, Philips, Siemens, EMI, General Electric, RCA, CBS, and MCA.

NOTES TO CHAPTER 2

[1] C. H. Sterling and T. R. Haight, *The Mass Media: Aspen Institute Guide to Communication Industry Trends*, Praeger, New York, 1978, p. xxxii.

[2] N. Garnham, "The Economics of the U.S. Motion Picture Industry," Report to the Commission of the European Communities, Strasbourg, 1980, p. 2.

[3] OECD, *Impact of Multinational Enterprises on National Scientific and Technical Capacities*, OECD, Paris, 1977, p. 7.

[4] C. J. Hamelink, *The Corporate Village*, IDOC, Rome, 1977.

[5] A number of significant information corporations are privately held and do not publicly disclose their operational figures, such as *Reader's Digest*, Hearst Co., and Hughes Aircraft.

[6] As one will observe a number of corporations had sales below the $100 million mark. They are considered to be so crucial in their sector that they could not be left out.

[7] For newsagency history, see, i.a., F. Reyes Matta, *La Evolución Historica de las Agencias Transnacionales de Noticias haca la Dominación*, ILET, Mexico, 1976; H. Höhne, *Report über Nachrichtenagenturen*, Part 2, Nomos, Baden-Baden, 1977.

[8] T. Varis, "Der Einfluss transnationaler Konzerne auf die Kommunikation," in J. Becker (ed.), *Free Flow of Information*, Gemeinschaftswerk der Evangelischen Publizistik, Frankfurt, 1979, p. 70.

[9] T. Guback, "International Circulation of Theatrical Motion Pictures and Television Programming." Paper for Conference, World Communications: Decisions for the Eighties, Annenberg School of Communications, Philadelphia, May 1980, p. 10.

[10] N. Janus and R. Roncagliolo, "A Survey of the Transnational Structure of the Mass Media and Advertising," Report for the UN Centre on Transnational Corporations, Mexico, July 1978, p. 126.

[11] Data from "Transnational Corporations in World Development: A Re-Examination," United Nations, New York, March 1978.

[12] Calculated from 1976 gross income figures for the largest U.S. ad agencies, *Advertising Age*, April 17, 1978.

[13] "The World's Top 50 Computer Import Markets" (1975), in *Datamation*, March 1978.

[14] *Variety*, July 11, 1979; T. Guback, "Theatrical Film," In B. Compaine (ed.) *Who owns the media*, Knowledge Industry Publications, White Plains, New York, 1979, p. 219 a.f.

[15] OECD, op.cit., p. 20.

[16] C. J. Hamelink, "Informatics en een Nieuwe Informatie Orde," in *Massa-communicatie*, VII/3, 1979, p. 94.

[17] A. H. Solomon (Telecommunications Sciences Division of Arthur D. Little) in a speech at Innisbrook (U.S.), quoted by *De Automatiseringsgids*, April 24, 1980.

[18] "The Foundations of United States Information Policy," U.S. Government Submission to the OECD Conference on Information, Computer and Communications Policy, Paris, October 6-8, 1980, p. 10.

[19] For information industry and the military, see, i.a., H. I. Schiller, *Mass Communications and American Empire*, Beacon Press, Boston, 1971 (chapters 3, 4 and 5); idem, *The Mind Managers*, Beacon Press, Boston, 1973 (chapter 3); A. Mattelart, *Multinationales et systèmes de communication*, Editions Anthropos, Paris, 1976 (chapters 2 and 3); C. J. Hamelink, *De computersamenleving*, Anthos Baarn, 1980 (pp. 72-77).

[20] "Interlocking Directorates among the Major U.S. Corporations," A Study prepared by the Subcommittee on Reports, Accounting and Management of the U.S. Senate Committee on Governmental Affairs, January 1978, p. 102.

[21] ibid., p. 102.

[22] P. W. Bernstein, "Here Come the Superagencies," in *Fortune*, August 27, 1979, p. 46.

[23] N. Garnham, op.cit., p. 16, 17; P. Bächlin, *Ekonomische geschiedenis van de film*, Socialistische Uitgeverij, Nijmegen, 1977, p. 31; "The Film Council," in A. Mattelart and S. Siegelaub, *Communication and Class Struggle, An anthology*, Part I, International General, New York; International Mass Media Research Center, Bagnolet, France, 1979, p. 295.

[24] P. Bächlin, op.cit., p. 99.

[25] N. Garnham, op.cit., p. 17.

[26] S. Chapple and R. Garofalo, *Rock'n Roll is Here to Pay*, Nelson Hall, Chicago 1977, p. 92.

[27] OECD, op.cit., p. 9.

[28] ibid., p. 12.

[29] N. Garnham, op.cit., p. 19.

[30] ibid., p. 11.

[31] ibid., p. 24.

[32] *Variety*, January 10, 1979.

[33] Calculated from data in N. Garnham, op.cit.; *Variety*; T. Guback, op.cit.

[34] *Fortune*, April 23, 1979. Particularly responsible for this growth has been rock music. Its latest blend with soul into "disco sound" accounts in some estimates for over 25% of the record market.

[35] *Variety*, February 21, 1979.

[36] *Billboard*, September 30, 1978.

[37] N. Janus and R. Roncagliolo, op.cit., p. 124.

[38] ibid., p. 176.

[39] A. Mattelart, "The Geopolitics of Paper," in A. Mattelart and S. Siegelaub, op.cit., p. 305.

[40] J. Becker, "The Paper Crisis in Peripheral Capitalism," In *Peace and the Sciences*, 1/1979, p. 14.

[41] Cf, i.a., J. H. Dunning and R. B. Pearce, "Profitability and Performance of the World's Largest Industrial Companies," *Financial Times*, London, 1975, p. 48.

[42] J. F. Magee, Testimony in hearings before the Subcommittee on International Operations of the U.S. Senate Committee on Foreign Relations, June 1977, p. 245.

[43] see note 9, Chapter 1.

[44] H. Geller, quoted in *Transnational Data Report*, vol. 3, no. 1, May 1980, p. 7.

[45] *Advertising Age*, April 30, 1980.

[46] A. Pearce, "Telematics Market Heating Up," *Telecommunications*, May 1980, p. 16.

[47] Worldwide DP revenues were calculated from *Datamation* data in June 1978 and July 1980.*

[48] A. Pearce, op.cit., p. 10.

[49] *Advertising Age*, March 24, 1980; R. Coen, v.p. McCann Erickson in *International Herald Tribune*, June 11, 1980.

[50] McCann Erickson, "Annual Report," 1975.

[51] *Fortune*, April 23, 1979, p. 60.

[52] ibid., p. 60.

[53] *Variety*, August 29, 1979.

[54] The special outer space effects for the film Star Trek are expected to make this an over 42 million dollar production (*Variety*, August 29, 1979). F. E. Rosenfelt in a speech before the Annual Convention of the National Association of Theatre Owners, October, 1980.

[55] See reference to U.S. Commerce Department Annual Outlook in footnote 47.

[56] R&D figures for the information industry stem from corporations' annual reports, the *Business Week* "R&D Scoreboard" and the April 1980 special R&D section of *International Herald Tribune*. Worldwide R&D expenditures for information technology were estimated on the basis of data in C. Norman, "Knowledge and Power: The Global Research and Development Budget," *Worldwatch Paper* No. 31, July 1979.

[57] The R&D figure is the price of stock/R&D ratio. Information from R. J. Burger, stockbroker with Dean Witter Reynolds Inc.

* Data on the U.S. DP market stem from an advance excerpt of the U.S. Commerce Department (Bureau of Industrial Economics) Annual U.S. Industrial Outlook. Quoted in *Computerworld*, Feb. 16, 1981.

[58] A case in point is the respectable U.K. newspaper, *The Times*, Although a loss prone venture there may be interested parties in its takeover due to the political prestige involved. An example is also the U.K. Sunday paper, *The Observer*, that was rescued in 1976 by an oil company, Atlantic Richfield. This was mainly because the chief executive of the company, Robert Anderson, was impressed with the idea of saving a world famous newspaper.

[59] *Forbes*, October 1, 1979.

[60] A. Robinson, "Metamorphosis in the Media," *Financial Times*, November 18, 1977.

[61] P. Wilson-Smith, *The Times*, Feb. 24, 1981.

[62] Report 15 for the International Commission for the Study of Communication Problems (in the series on newsagencies), p. 118.

[63] P. Wilson-Smith, op.cit.

[64] Calculations from data in i.a. P. Harris, "News Dependence," Unpublished report to UNESCO, 1977, and studies by J. Hart, CIESPAL, ILET, and A. Hester.

[65] Information in "Kwaliteitskranten en hun financieringskapitaal," Thesis by J. de la Haye and G. Tijhuis, University of Amsterdam, April 1978.

[66] *Business Week*, August 27, 1979, p. 94.

3

The Importance of Information for the Banking Industry

Chapter 2 has shown that the information industry needs considerable financing for its research and development, for production and marketing costs. It also pointed to the sales of financial information as an important source of revenue for some sectors in the information industry. Moreover, it indicated that several information corporations through their financial service subsidiaries actually perform banking operations.

These observations provide the basis for a further exploration of relations between information and banking industries.

Bankers have long ago begun to understand the importance of information for the effective operating of their trade. It is hardly a coincidence that the first newspaper in Europe was published by the 16th century Augsburg bankers family of the Fuggers. In the 19th century (1856) the bankers Heinrich Bernhard Rosenthal and Leopold Sonnemann started the *Frankfurter Geschäftsbericht* for stock exchange information: the predecessor of the *Frankfurter Handelszeitung* which is today's *Frankfurter Allgemeine Zeitung.*

Banker Nathan Rothschild organized a private carrier pigeon service through which he obtained early information about Napoleon's defeat at Waterloo (1815). This enabled him to make stock market decisions before his competitors and to conduct profitable transactions with English state securities.

Bankers were among the first clients of the 19th century international newsagencies, and still today they buy the agencies' commodity: money-market information.

In the second half of the 20th century, bankers recognize that their effective operation has become dependent upon information flows across national borders. As Citibank vice-president R. B. White testifies, "Today's high transaction volumes and geographic spread have introduced communications problems that demand sophisticated technological solutions. This is why we are primarily dependent upon electronic media for international communications, both in providing services to our customers and in administrative communication between our branches. Not too long ago, our international business was transacted mainly by mail, with some use of telegraphic services to initiate funds transfers. But the complexity of international business today places a premium on speed and accuracy. Exchange rates and commodity prices fluctuate rapidly. Competitive bids are made for short supplies. Our customer often needs credits or transfers completed and advices issued in a matter of hours, not days."[1]

Assistant vice-president L. Van Kleeck of the Arizona Bank adds to this, "A banking question or inquiry is almost always urgent enough for the customer to want an answer immediately, and that requires good telephone service. Customer access is critically important to a commercial bank."[2] This makes telecommunications "an essential part of contemporary banking operations," as J. Blodgett of Valley National Bank asserts.[3] Since banks' telecommunications have to be fast there is increasing interest in computerized communications systems. Whereas international telex calls may take some 20 seconds for the connection to be established, computer systems can connect their users in 4 seconds.

The bankers' viewpoint can be summed up in a statement by R. Walker (vice-president of Continental Illinois Bank), "As an international bank, our business is entirely dependent upon the free flow of instantaneous communication."[4] In concluding his testimony before the U.S. House of Representatives' Subcommittee on Government Information and Individual Rights on March 13, 1980, Walker left no doubts. "We at Continental Bank are convinced that any regulation, legislation, tariff, or tax which could inhibit the free flow of data will seriously affect not only U.S. banking business abroad, but will stunt the continuing development and maturation of international trade, which we need in the interdependent economic world in which we all find ourselves in this latter part of the Twentieth Century."[5]

"Barclays has always meant banking, but today it means a great deal more."

from an advertisement

The functions banks perform are strongly information-related. This means that they imply the necessity to purchase *technical equipment* through which information can be processed and transmitted, to buy and sell *information as a commodity*, and to use services of operators of information *linking systems*.

The key function of banking is the mediating between borrowers and lenders of money. This involves the depositing, transferring, and demanding of money. Money, however, in whatever form, is merely the symbolic representation of its holders' assets. As such it is an information carrier and its transactions are information acts. Related to the money activity are a series of services that center around information. Banks need to respond to customers' requests for information about their account balances, foreign currencies, interest rates, bond markets, etc. Banks, for their overall operations, need "minute-by-minute intelligence from the money markets across the world,"[6] and for their normal lending business they need "information about the political and economic basis of the various trading areas of the world."[7]

Since commercial banks evidently want to attract customers, they also have to market themselves: another informational activity in which they have become increasingly involved over the past years. This is, i.a., due to a considerable diversification of banking services into new areas. "Such activities include revolving, medium-term loans, special services for the insurance and investment needs of corporate clients as well as serving in other capacities, including advice on mergers and commodity trade."[8] As the Barclays' advertisement suggests, banking today "means a great deal more," it also includes travel services to the general public. For the large transnational customers, services include: the provision of macro-economic and marketing data, provision of information on exchange controls, taxes and investment regulations, recommendations concerning local business connections, leasing of physical assets, management of profit-sharing or expansion systems.[9] As indicated before, the information activities of the banks are performed through the three categories into which the information industry can be divided.

THE PURCHASE OF
INFORMATION TECHNICAL EQUIPMENT

Since banks' telecommunications networks have to be fast, reliable, and efficient, banks are installing computerized business telephone systems. An example is the Arizona Bank, with its ROLM system that "will greatly expand customer service, cut instate toll charges up to 90 percent, allow for use of the bank's potential development of a proprietary microwave system for extra cost savings, and even enable customers to summon emergency first aid for the bank's automatic teller machine network."[10] Upon completion in 1981, the bank will have a full satellite operation linking its 84 branches spread throughout the state of Arizona.

> "In our lifetime we may see electronic transactions virtually eliminate the need for cash".
>
> T. J. Watson Jr., President of IBM, 1965

Paper money, invented in the 17th century has to give way increasingly to other media. In the 1950s, checks became widely used in replacing cash payment. During the 1960's, credit cards began to take over, first in the U.S., and later in other industralized countries. These "plastic promissory notes" are according to C. Evans "the first nails in the coffin of traditional financial methods."[11] In the early 70's an annual $5 billion in credit card transactions was reported in the U.S. In 1979 the U.K. Banking Information Services estimates that 7 million people in Britain hold such cards. The widespread use of credit cards led to the need for banks to install authorization systems, such as First National Bank of Chicago's Infoswitch system for the handling of between 5000–12,000 authorization calls on a routine day.[12] Watson's foresight has turned out to be correct: the 1980s will see that increasingly the transfer of funds will take place in the form of digital data flowing between computers.

"Since 1975 the financial community has been buzzing over the prospect of an electronic system that may substitute for much of the paper-based money transfer system."[13] In 1978 *Fortune* reported that financial institutions have installed an estimated 21,000 electronic funds transfer (EFT) terminals throughout the U.S. These include some 7,700 automated teller machines, which not only transfer funds electronically, but also accept cash deposits and provide cash for withdrawal.[14] In 1979 European banks spent an estimated $1 billion for automated equipment and this is expected to increase to some $6 billion in 1990. Sixty percent of this will be spent for terminals at the teller's windows. The use of terminals by European banks is expected to grow with 36% annually in the period 1980–1983.[15]

EFT systems are information media for a variety of financial transactions, such as funds transfers between banks, funds transfers between banks' computers and other institutions' computers, cash dispensing or depositing, and automatic payment systems in retail shops.

EFT is labor saving for the banks; it increases the speed of money transfer, speeds up the clearing time for checks, and attracts customers. "Many marketing people in banking argued that terminal-based services brought increased customer convenience, a wider variety of services, and eventually more deposits."[16]

BUYING AND SELLING INFORMATION AS A COMMODITY

Banks compose political and economic profiles of the pertinent trading areas of the world for internal use or for utilization by clients. Such profiles are based on information collected through diverse sources such as national central banks, trade journals, banks' analysts, and the international news agencies. As indicated, some of them (particularly Reuters) provide a wide scale of financial and economic data in specialized services to which the banking community subscribes.

In a survey conducted for the present study among member banks of the Society of Worldwide Interbank Financial Telecommunications (S.W.I.F.T.) the following types of information services were indicated:

- newsletters
- booklets
- periodical economic and financial bulletins
- economic surveys and forecasts
- securities information systems
- foreign lending information services
- special reports and reviews
- financial databases

Some banks choose imaginative formats for publication, such as Citibank's "Sound of the Economy"—an audio-cassette service. Examples of periodical publications include the monthly *World Financial Markets* by Morgan Guaranty Trust Company, the bi-weekly *International Finance* by the Economics Group of the Chase Manhattan Bank, and the quarterly *Citiviews* distributed to Citi corporations' investors. Most of such services are distributed without charge.

Banks collect data on countries through teams of researchers sent on missions and through their local branches. This leads to the composing of countries' risk profiles. It may involve the forecasting of political developments.

In discussions with representatives of one of the largest banks in the world, the Chase Manhattan Corp., plans were indicated for an extensive database on 120 countries with risk reports, i.a., containing information on potential civil disorders, tax changes, expropriation measures, and foreign support for opposition movements. The database would be accessible for subscribers willing to pay a fee of $25,000 per year.[17]

The richness of data they collect leads one banking official to comment "we know more about Brazil's economy than its own government."[18] This is indeed very likely, since the banks collect and process information with material and staff resources not available to most state authorities.

Banks also buy information; for example, from credit bureaus, the private data banks that provide information on individuals to subscribers such as department stores, automobile dealers, etc. In the early 1970s the largest bureau was TRW Credit Data of Long Beach, California. It provided some 12 million credit reports to 7,000 subscribers annually and held records on some 30 million individuals.

Banks also buy information from databases. In a survey by R. H. Veith about half of the respondents said to use one or more commercial, computerized databases for economic/financial information.

Most frequently used databases were the *U.S. Federal Reserve* Flow of Funds, U.S. Weekly Banking and FRBSF, the *World Bank's* World Debt Tables, the *IMF* Balance of Payments and International Finance, *Chase Econometrics'* Foreign Exchange, *Merill Lynch's* Merril Lynch Economics and Spot Rates-Currency of *Extel Statistics.*[19] Reuters' Economic Services was used daily by 5 percent of the respondents. In the survey conducted for this study this percentage was 15.

Banks also buy services such as computer timesharing, datatransmission or software packages from companies like General Electric and Tymshare. These computer service companies count many of the largest banks among their clients. Tymshare, serving over a thousand banks announced in early 1981 the creation of the International Banking Information System that will offer up-to-the minute profiles of international banking activities.

Banks are also involved in the selling of computer services, like Citibank which is moving into a variety of data-processing activities. Citibank has targeted three distinct businesses. As a systems house, the bank is combining its own programs and software with someone else's hardware and marketing the system to end-users. As a remote computing-services company, it is selling time on its own computers to outside customers. And as a software house, Citibank is selling applications software packages to customers who will run them on their own computers.

As Citibank vice-president R. B. White comments, "In the long run we would like to represent 10% of Citicorp's profits."[20] In 1976 Citibank began selling its computer services externally with revenues between $100 and 150 million. In 1977 the DP branch Citishare was set up. Citishare offers a wide range of financial packages, time-sharing services and database services to the industry. While attempting to secure approval from the federal government to spin off Citishare, the bank began acquiring DP-related companies. In 1979 it acquired Lexar Business Communications and in 1980 it bought 7 computer services companies. The bank also began establishing new subsidiaries, such as BHC Resources Inc., involved in office automation services, and Citicorp Information Services for the sales of minicomputers to bank holding companies. Its DP activities make Citibank the 26th largest independent computer services company in the U.S.[21]

The Chase Manhattan Bank has by far the most extensive investments in information services. In 1978 one estimate attributed $2.5 billion revenues to Chase Manhattan's economic information services with a growth rate of 30 percent yearly.[22]

Chase Manhattan owns three important subsidiaries in information services.

Chase Econometrics Associates Inc. is the largest U.S. firm in economic forecasting. It deals with such questions as which markets will expand next year and which will contract? How will commodity prices fluctuate over the next several years, and where will interest rates be next year?

Chase World Information Corporation provides research, advisory services, and publications for the international business community. It focuses on analysis and consulting for new markets in the Middle East, Eastern Europe, and China.

Interactive Data Corporation is a computer services organization which provides financial and economic data and information processing services to financial institutions, corporations, and governments.[23]

The past years have seen an important increase in banks' spending on advertising through various media. Banks have left their traditionally guarded positions to some degree and have moved into public promoting of their services. Sharon Baum, advertising director of Chemical Bank, comments on this development, "Today, equating an international funds transfer service with a detergent is not only appropriate but necessary in light of a competitive banking environment."[24]

Particularly in the late 1970s, the ways in which financial institutions promote themselves has undergone drastic changes. And, as an *Advertising Age* editorial views it, "From a marketing point of view, banks have come a long way, but their need for advertising and marketing expertise is about to become even more acute." Record high interest rates and new competitors (like in the U.S. from Savings and Loans and other thrift institutions) is making it increasingly difficult to attract or keep depositors.[25]

Also, the diversification of services makes more advertising essential. "Marketing has become an important factor in bank operation as banks are offering a virtual laundry list of services, each of which appeals to a different segment of readers and each of which would justify a special advertising program," says Newspaper Advertising Bureau marketing vice-president U. Grava, as he stimulates bankers to more intensive use of newspaper advertising.[26] Also, the ways in which banking services are delivered to the consumers ask for more advertising. The automated teller machines, payments via telephone, retail sale terminals, all demand extensive educational and image advertising. It is not only individual banks that respond to these challenges, the U.S. banking community, represented by the American Bankers Association, has decided to campaign collectively for a more competitive position of the commercial banks. On May 13, 1979 the Association launched a series of TV spots, prepared by Burnett Co., that suggest that banks "have the answers" to all kinds of financial problems.[27] A striking aspect of bankers' advertising is the increasing use of premiums as tools for promoting their services. Premiums promised to prospective clients range from crystal glasses to videotape recorders, gold chains, and voyages. In 1978, U.S. financial institutions spent some $147 million on such incentives.[28]

Even the cautious British bankers have begun promotion campaigns aimed at some 11 million youngsters that not yet have banking accounts. This indicates, not only competition among the U.K. banks, but also the rapid invasion of U.S. banks. In 1980, Lloyds Bank offered young married couples discounts on such goods as TV sets, toasters, and dishwashers. This promotion was supported with $230,000 advertising in the newspapers designed by McCann Erickson.

National Westminster spends $3,450,000 on advertising through the sponsoring of a popular cricket competition.

Midland Bank spent over $5,750,000 in 1979 on advertising, and Barclays promoted its Barclaycard, financial services, and personal banking services with a $6,440,000 budget.[29]

U.S. bank marketing in 1977 was calculated by *Advertising Age* to amount to $692,668,600.[30] The average expenditure for marketing by banks with over $1 billion in deposits was $1,589,400. Most of the marketing budgets were spent on newspaper and radio advertising. According to the Newspaper Advertising Bureau, financial advertising in newspapers increased by 30% from 1977 to 1978 and was ahead of other retail groups.[31] In the first half of 1980 such advertising surged another 37.5 percent and amounted to $186.7 million.[32]

In its 1978 annual report, the German Bank für Gemeinwirtschaft writes, "BFG advertising specifies not only the services offered to private customers but also the respective terms and conditions. Our slogan, 'The more you know about banks, the better for us,' reflects our wish that the consumer should make critical comparisons between our services and those offered by other banks." The BFG calls this "informatory advertising."

A sample of banking advertisements shows how banks inform the consumer about themselves and their competitors.

Comparative advertising can be found in the full-page ads in New York newspapers by Manufacturers Hanover, in which the bank campaigns against its rival, Citibank. The advertisement suggests that Citibank, which claims "it never sleeps," was caught napping when it continued paying a lower interest percentage than recent banking regulation allowed: "We caught the Citi napping."

Ranking among the world's ten largest banks, the Dresdner Bank gave the public its essential financial figures in 1978 and explained how successful its international operations had been.

The Japanese Daiwa Bank claims to be unique in making acceptance of social responsibility an integral part of its banking service. Its integration of banking services are meant "to fulfill our social responsibility consistent with society's needs in a contemporary environment."

Dutch Rabobank likes to see itself as inspired by 17th century painter Rembrandt: "The country which inspired Rembrandt's internationally acclaimed masterpieces has inspired the Rabobank to create services of worldwide importance." The bank also claims credibility, since it is rooted in agricultural financing for over 80 years.

East New York Savings informs the consumer that "finally a bank offers you incentives somewhat more appealing than a tacky little toaster."

The British Midland Bank advises the London underground passengers to "come and talk to the listening bank."

Banks address themselves to the higher social strata in their advertising. They compare themselves to medical services; they go after the Fortune top 500 or exploit new customer groups such as women. With regard to the latter, the Interbank consortium promoting its Master Card concedes, "When it comes to women, banks still haven't come of age. It's a man-oriented industry. When a bank thinks of a household, it still thinks of the man of the house," according to the editor of the Credit Card Marketing newsletter.

E. Younger, Interbank Senior Vice-President for marketing, in explaining the campaign that will take more than one-third of Master Charge's $9.5 million advertising budget states: "We want to stimulate banks to look at the women's market in general, and, not incidentally, to push Master Charge more aggressively."[33]

INFORMATION LINKING SERVICES

Telecommunications has become a vital part of today's banking operations. International banking uses telephone, cable, and telex services via underseas cables or satellites through leased channels from international private telecommunication carriers (such as RCA, AT&T, and IT&T) and national public utilities (PTTs). In order to provide dependable communication services they have also developed private communication networks that handle large volumes of transborder financial data flows. Most of the data are still transported in rather traditional ways. Increasingly, however, with the rapid convergence of computer and telecommunications technologies, computerized data networks are being created that carry enormous volumes of information rapidly and reliably in the form of digital signals. Transmission through such networks commenced in the 1950s with the first circuits for defense-systems and airline reservations. Their decisive development started in the 1970s and is expected to grow expansively throughout the 1980s and 1990s. (Table 33 gives a survey of the various applications of these transnational computer-communication systems).

Present day transborder data flows contain mainly information of technical/scientific, economic, and military nature. Although no definite information is as yet available, it can be safely assumed that financial data account for an important share in these data flows. Bankers have certainly recognized the far-reaching possibilities of handling their services through such computer networks.

A recent survey among leading banks indicates that bankers estimate their information exchange activities to consist of:

- 28% intradepartmental communications;
- 25% interdepartmental communications;
- 22% interbank communications, and
- 21% communications with clients.[34]

The same survey shows that in bank-to-bank telecommunications during any normal working day the telephone is used 34% of the time, the telex 32% of the time, the computer 9%, and facsimile 4% of the time.

The responding bankers rate the importance of telecommunications equipment in the following order:

1. telex,
2. telephone,
3. mail,
4. computer,
5. international travel,
6. facsimile.

Asked to rate the importance of telecommunications means in six years time, the outcome is:

1. computer,
2. telephone,
3. telex,
4. international travel,
5. mail,
6. facsimile.[35]

In a survey conducted for the present study, a sample from the largest international banks indicated that 73% of respondents rated the telex as the most important telecommunications equipment, 58% of the respondents said that they made a combined use of telex and computer. In 23% of the responses the computer was mentioned as the most important communications medium. In all cases the telephone rated highest.[36] In 1980, the major U.S. banks expected to spend more than $1 billion annually for telephone services alone.[37]

The need for international telecommunications networks has drastically increased with the transnationalization of banking. During the 1960s and the beginning of the 1970s, U.S. banks, followed by the top Westeuropean and Japanese banks, spread worldwide. A major factor was the growth of international trade. This led to the increase in financial transactions, since a large part of global exports was financed with trade credits arranged by the major banks. Another key factor was the internationalization of production and the concurrent increase in overseas investments by the large transnational industrial corporations. This made the system of doing financial business from the home office or through correspondence banks inadequate. "Banks had to provide more information on the chances of business abroad, and they could only provide such information if they themselves were represented abroad.[38] This gave rise to the establishment of representative offices in foreign countries. These soon turned out to have an important weakness because they could do no business themselves and had to continue to rely on the correspondence banks. At present the most important forms of transnationalization of banks are: international branch networks, international banking groups, and international consortia banks.[39]

The growth of the banks' transnationalization can be illustrated with the U.S. case. In 1960, only 8 banks had foreign branches, totalling some $3.5 billion in assets.[40] In 1978 far more than 100 banks had 761 foreign branches with assets amounting to $306 billion.[41] A good example of today's transnational banking provides "the most truly international bank,"[42] Citibank, with its global network of over 2,000 foreign offices in over 100 countries. The transnationalization has turned out to be very profitable; in 1976, the 5 largest U.S. banks receive 40% of their profits from overseas lending. Chase Manhattan Bank derives 78% of its profits from foreign operations.

As a U.S. Congressional study commented in 1977, "the spectacular expansion of international lending has been critical to maintain a steady growth of earning for major U.S. banks."[43] To this observation, a report by Salomon Brothers adds that between 1970 and 1975 some 95% of the growth of earnings for the top 13 U.S. banks came from overseas operations.[44] Table 34 compares foreign revenues for the top U.S. banks in 1970 and 1977.

It must be noted here that the transnationalization of banking concurs with a strong degree of concentration in banking. The capital intensive information technology is one among the important contributing factors. The large-scale application and development of international telecommunications networks gives incomparable advantages for large banks as against their smaller competitors. The large banks that resulted from the many mergers in the 1960s and early 1970s in U.S. and Western Europe had the necessary strong domestic base to become the leading international banks. In 1976, the 20 largest U.S. banks accounted for 82% of the foreign offices and in 1977 the top 12 banks accounted for 68% of total foreign assets.[45]

To adequately respond to the communications needs created by this transnationalization, the banks created networks for their individual use and for interbank use.

Examples of the first category are the Chase Manhattan private communications network (see Figure 8) and Citibank's GLOBECOM. The latter stands for the network of leased channels that interconnect the overseas branches of Citibank in some 100 countries. More than 300,000 transmissions per month pass through computer switches in London, Bahrain, Hong Kong, and New York. Most of the circuits are low speed telegraphic circuits. Store and forward switching is the primary means of transmission. Some of the circuits are SVD circuits, and voice channels on those circuits are used for administrative communication among the different branches. Citibank spends an estimated $40 million yearly on its international telecommunications operations.[46]

Examples of the second category are the European network EUREX and the global network S.W.I.F.T. (see Figures 9 and 10).

EUREX goes back to 1973 when a group of 69 banks from 14 countries explored the possibility of setting up an automated trading system for international bonds. EUREX SA was incorporated in the Grand Duchy of

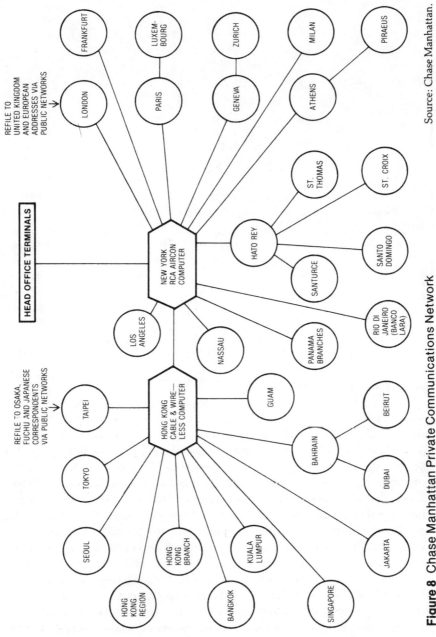

Figure 8 Chase Manhattan Private Communications Network

Source: Chase Manhattan.

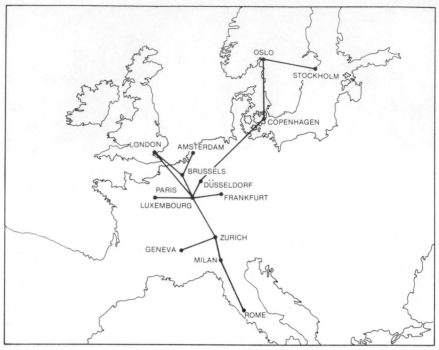

Figure 9 Eurex Network

Source: J. P. Chamoux, L'Information Sans Frontière, Paris: La Documentation Francaise, 1980, p. 162.

Luxembourg in September 1977 and became operational in late 1978. It consists of a network of international leased lines connecting most of the European financial centers with the key processing unit based in Luxembourg. It has on-line links with the clearing houses, and its purpose is to cover the whole range of information, trading, and back office services for the Eurobond market. As D. Grimwood, a director of EUREX, explains, "It provides for free dialogue trading where a dealer is able to have direct contact with a market maker. Telephone trades may be booked through the system at reduced cost and in addition, the computer will accept orders given by telex. Much of the information provided is closely related to the dealing function. For example, the system supplies a market maker with confidential in-house information which shows the position and cost of each quoted bond, details of recent transactions, yields and conversion premiums, and other relevant details. All participants have access to indicative quotations, details of specific bonds, new issues, general market news and a range of related items of interests."[47]

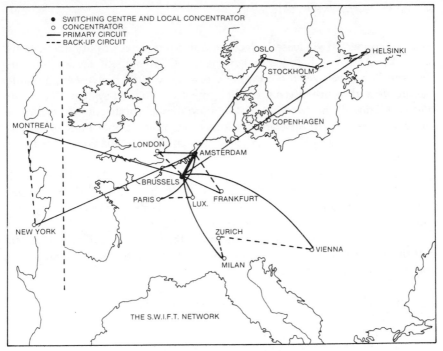

Figure 10 The Network

Source: General Information Brochure S.W.I.F.T., Third Edition, January 1978.

The hardware and software for the network has been developed by IBM.*

S.W.I.F.T. is the Society for Worldwide Interbank Financial Telecommunications. The idea for S.W.I.F.T. was born in the late 1960s when a group of large Westeuropean banks studied the possibility of improved international transaction procedures and came to the conclusion that international banking needed an accurate, rapid, safe, and standardized funds transfer system. As a result of the study and the positive response from the banks, the major Westeuropean, Canadian, and U.S. banks established S.W.I.F.T. in May 1973. Four years later, in May 1977, the network became operational. By then almost $1 billion was spent for the network and equipment was procured from Burroughs, ICL, and General Automation. In 1980, S.W.I.F.T. was expected to carry 250.000 messages (of each some 250 characters) daily through its system with which different types of terminals

* In early 1981 it was announced that EUREX went into liquidation due to lack of business.

could be connected via leased telecommunications lines or public telephone networks. As S.W.I.F.T. general manager, C. Reuterskiöld, describes it, "For the first time ever the banking world now has its own fast, reliable responsive and secure international payment transaction system."[48] An important feature of the system is that it guarantees absolute confidentiality of message transfer with all transmissions over international lines being encrypted. Encryption keys at the ends of each line are changed at random intervals.

S.W.I.F.T. connects over 700 banks in 26 countries through operating centers in Belgium, the Netherlands, and the U.S. Transactions processed fall into 4 main categories: customer transfers, bank transfers, foreign exchange confirmations, and loan/deposit confirmations.

In the survey carried out for this study the responding banks indicated that their international transmissions were divided into the following categories:

- funds transfers: 40% (60% of these were bank transfers)
- letters of credit: 20%
- administrative messages: 15%
- foreign exchange: 13%
- information exchange (queries, answers, advice): 12%

The volume of transmissions per day varies greatly between the banks, from 100 to over 300,000. For the banks in the sample an average can be constructed that would amount to 50,000 transmissions per day.

Also, the annual budget for telecommunications equipment and services shows large variations. The average amount, $18.5 million, gives some idea as to what a major international bank might spend per year.

There can be no doubt about the fact that banks rank among the most important users of information linking services. This has led bankers to realize that their operations form a vital element in the future growth of the telecommunications sector. According to a representative of the American Bankers Association, the telecommunications manufacturers and operators now "recognize that we are a power in the telecommunications industry." And flatly, he adds, "We are flattered, but we also intend to use our newfound power. We're not going to throw it away."[49]

SUMMARY

The various functions that banks perform are strongly information-related. The increasing importance of information is due to the character of today's banking operations in which banking has virtually become the storing, processing, and distributing of information. Banks are important purchasers of the technical equipment through which information can be processed and transmitted. Banks are also increasingly involved with the buying and selling of information services and of information as a commodity. Banking has become dependent upon sophisticated communications networks and banks are among the largest users of information linking services. Finance and information are thus converging areas.

NOTES TO CHAPTER 3

[1] R. B. White in his testimony during the hearings before the Subcommittee on International Operations of the U.S. Senate Committee on Foreign Relations, Washington, 1977, p. 247.

[2] *Telecommunications*, Feb. 1980, p. 79.

[3] *Telecommunications*, April 1980, p. 61.

[4] Testimony by R. E. L. Walker before the Subcommittee on Government Information and Individual Rights of the U.S. House of Representatives Committee on Government Operations, March 13, 1980.

[5] ibid.

[6] ibid.

[7] ibid.

[8] R. Väyrynen, "Concentration and Internationalization in Banking." *Research Report*, Series D, Department of Political Science, University of Turku, No. 4, 1975, p. 47.

[9] U.S. Department of Commerce, "Current Developments in U.S. International Service Industries," U.S. Govt. Printing Office, Washington, D.C. March 1980, p. 36.

[10] *Telecommunications*, Feb. 1980, p. 78.

[11] C. Evans, *The Mighty Micro*, Victor Gollancz, London 1979, p. 131.

[12] *Telecommunications*, Feb. 1980, p. 48.

[13] J. B. Benton, "Electronic Funds Transfer: Pitfalls and Payoffs," *Harvard Business Review*, Vol. 55, No. 4, July-August 1977, p. 16.

[14] S. Rose, "The Unexpected Fallout from Electronic Banking," *Fortune*, April 24, 1979, p. 83.
For Europe, see P.A. Management Consultants' Report, "Informatics in European Banks in 1980," Brussels 1980.

[15] Report by Frost & Sullivan, London. Quoted in *Computable*, Nov. 14, 1980, p. 2.

[16] J. B. Benton, op.cit., p. 17.

[17] Interviews with executives from Chase Manhattan Corp. in New York, carried out during March 1978.

[18] See 17.

[19] R. H. Veith, Information transfer in international banking networks, an attitude survey in which 45 bankers from U.S. banks and from French, German and Japanese bank branches in New York participated. Survey results were reported in R. H. Veith, Multinational Computer Nets, D. C. Heath, Lexington, 1981. For database use see pp. 72–79.

[20] R. B. White quoted in *Business Week*, August 4, 1980, p. 54.

[21] R. Emmett, "Citishare or Citigrab?", *Datamation*, March 1981, pp. 46-48.

[22] See 17.

[23] Description from *Chase Information Services Guide*.

[24] *Advertising Age*, section on Financial Advertising, Feb. 5, 1979.

[25] *Advertising Age*, editorial, Oct. 20, 1980, p. 16.

[26] *Editor & Publisher*, Sept. 23, 1978, p. 20.

[27] *Advertising Age*, May 14, 1979, p. 4.

[28] The *Incentive Marketing Report* lists banks and savings and loans as the ninth largest user of incentives, *Advertising Age*, January 28, 1980, p. 46. When interstate banking becomes legally a reality in the U.S. it is expected that advertising spending by the largest banks could increase tenfold. *Advertising Age*, Jan. 19, 1981, p. 6.

[29] *Advertising Age*, July 28, 1980, p. 24.

[30] *Advertising Age*, July 10, 1978.

[31] *Editor & Publisher*, April 14, 1979.

[32] *Editor & Publisher*, Sept. 6, 1980.

[33] J. Levine, "Interbank Touts Clout for Women," *Advertising Age*, June 1979, p. 1, 80.

[34] R. H. Veith, op.cit., p. 85.

[35] R. H. Veith, op.cit., p. 66.

[36] The survey was carried out with the questionnaire that can be found as appendix: II. The questionnaire was sent to a random sample of 100 member banks of the Society for Worldwide Interbank Financial Telecommunication (SWIFT). This was done during 1978 and 1979. Thirty six banks filled out the questionnaire. Another ten gave information of a more general nature. Most banks preferred not to be quoted by name in the presentation of the results.

[37] *Telecommunications*, April 1980, p. 56.

[38] G. Junne, "Multinational Banks, the State and International Integration." In K. von Beyme (ed), *German Political Systems*, London 1976, p. 120.

[39] ibid.

[40] Data from U.S. House of Representatives, Committee on Banking, "Financial Instititions and the Nation's Economy," Washington 1976,; and *Financial Times*, June 6, 1978.

[41] U.S. Department of Commerce, op.cit., p. 35.

[42] Description by the *New York Times*, quoted in H. W. Wachtel, "The New Gnomes: Multinational Banks in the Third World," Washington 1977, p. 8.

[43] Quoted in the *Financial Times*, June 6, 1978.

[44]Salomon Brothers' report quoted in *CDE Handbook, Banking & Finance*, New York 1980, p. 43.

[45] *CDE Handbook,* op.cit., p. 43.

[46] Interview with Citibank executives in New York, carried out in March 1978.

[47]D. Grimwood in the *International Herald Tribune*, November 1979, p. 9S.

[48] In the foreword to SWIFT brochure.

[49] *Telecommunications,* April 1980, p. 53.

4

The Information
Industry
and its
Financiers

The preceding chapter suggests that bankers perceive of themselves as a crucial factor in the telecommunications sector of the information industry. This pertains also to other information industry sectors, as *Telecommunications* editor A. Pearce indicates, "All the bankers have to do now is to caucus-preferably well away from public and industry scrutiny and consider the many options available to them. These include taking a close look at the cable television industry, which is expanding rapidly at the local and intrastate level and can supply valuable broadband services to the banking community; Satellite Business Systems; Xerox's proposed XTEN; a tailor-made system provided by Rockwell or Exxon among others; a marriage of convenience with the giant, AT&T; or perhaps a combination of all."[1]

Bankers have an obvious interest in the equipment and services the information industry can deliver to them.*

Also, if the information industry can be described as a big, growing, and profitable business, it would be rather unusual if the banking community were not interested for investment purposes. Moreover, the capital intensive information industry needs to approach the financiers for the ex-

---

* Telecommunications and DP manufacturers count large banks among their important clients, such as Philips with the French Société Lyonnaise de Dépots and Crédit Industriel SA, Fujitsu with the Dai Ichi Kangyo Bank, Olivetti with the Banca Commerciale Italiana, and ICL with the Bank of Ireland.

pansion of its capital supply through credits, mergers, acquisitions, and the selling of stock.

There is an interdependence between financiers and the information industry that can be introduced with a series of illustrations.

The film industry is a good example. The rapid expansion in the early years of its existence is certainly due to the large support it received from finance capital procured through the banks. From the 1920s, Wall Street interests became prominent in the film industry. "The policy of financing their enterprises from their own profits which had sufficed for the earlier stages of the industry's development, proved inadequate in face of the vast new capital demands arising from the incomparably more expensive star-feature films and the theater acquisition campaigns of the postwar years."[2]

The eight major firms that came to control the film production and distribution in this period all developed close links with the large New York banks. Throughout the 1930s especially, two banking groups, the Morgan group and the Rockefeller group became the key financiers of the film industry. Directly or through related financiers they controlled the eight top film producers. The Morgan group was strongly related with Paramount and Warner Bros. The Rockefeller group with 20th Century Fox, Loew (MGM), and Radio Keith Orpheum (RKO).[3] The advent of the sound film reinforced the banks' control since they had considerable interest in those firms that owned the patents for sound equipment. The Morgan group had interests in Western Electric, which had contracts with Paramount, Universal, Warner Bros., Loew, 20th Century Fox, Warner, and United Artists. The Rockefeller group had interests in RCA, which had contracts with Columbia, RKO, 20th Century Fox, United Artists, and Warner.[4]

As a document in 1936 comments, "Today the movie world is one of the major industries in the country and the control of its leading units has been concentrated both directly and indirectly in the hands of the most powerful financial groups in the United States."[5]

The banks continue to be vital factors in the film industry today. It is precisely the combination of the need for large finance capital in film production and distribution and the high risks involved that results in bankers being primarily interested in the large firms and to see smaller independent efforts as speculative.[6]

As table 30 shows, the transnational film producers are all in the category of moderate to heavy borrowers of funds linking them to their main capital suppliers, such as MCA with the Bank of America, 20th Century Fox, Warner, and Columbia with the First National Bank of Boston.

In France banks have initiated special finance companies for their investments in film, UFIC (by the nationalized banks BNP, Crédit Lyonnais, CFC, BUP, and UFB) and SOFET-SOFIDI (by the private Banque Worms,

Banque Commerciale de Paris, CCF, and Crédit du Nord).[7] In Switzerland (Geneva) the Swiss banks have funded Lamitas, an international film financing company.

In London the branch office of the First National Bank of Chicago has mediated large loans to EMI and the Rank Organization. Most efforts to get British banks together to provide finance for film production continuously have not been very successful over the past years. The National Film Finance Consortium established in 1972 counts among its loans only $6 million from London banks. At the beginning of 1980, however, trade journal *Variety* reports that some London merchant banks are now showing interest in film investment activities.[8]

As was shown in the preceding chapter, banks have played an important role in the newspaper sector. They have also become involved in other branches of publishing. In France the Banque de Paris et des Pays Bas (Paribas) has been represented on the board of the publishing firm Hachette since its establishment, and today the bank is financing the firm's expansion in audiovisual production.[9]

The same bank has over the past year acquired considerable interests in large French paper producers, such as Groupement Européene de la Cellulose, La Chapelle-Darblay, and La Rochette-Cenpa. Another large financier, the Cie Financière de SUEZ, holds a considerable number of shares in Cellulose du Pin, Beghin and La Chapelle-Darblay, and Papeteries de Gascogne.[10]

The bank-industry link affects also the less traditional sectors of the information industry. For the DP sector it can rightly be argued that "the failure of several computer companies can be linked with the high capital expenditures required in order to operate successfully in the industry."[11]

In France, for example, DP business centers around three major participants: the state, the hardware manufacturers, and the banks. Out of the 12 major French DP firms, five are controlled by state-owned banks and three by private investment banks. As an OECD report comments, "The banks have come to realize the financial importance of these services."[12] In the Federal Republic of Germany the large Deutsche Bank acquired a 25% interest in the fast growing computer company Nixdorf in 1978.

To illustrate the interest of the financial community in the information industry, there is also the case of American Express. Table 35 gives some of American Express' direct and indirect interlocks with the information industry. During 1977 and 1978 American Express attempted to acquire McGraw Hill, the Book-of-the-Month Club, and Disney Productions. In the latter half of 1979 it agreed to pay $175 million for 50% of Warner Cable Corp., the cable subsidiary of Warner Communications Inc. "WCI has repeatedly touted the tremendous growth potential of the cable business, but in making the sale WCI got something more than money: a measure of respectability for the benefit of banks, underwriters and local governments that grant lucrative cable franchises."[13]

After having been rebuffed in other attempts, American Express now has an entry in a rapidly growing industry, Pay-TV, and, from all the signs, it is clear that its interest in the information industry does not end here.

In the U.S. it is not only the commercial banks and their trust departments that have shown interest in the information industry, but the investment banks are also keenly interested. Investment bankers are, in fact, the middlemen, the brokers for corporate borrowing. They advise their corporate clients on the sales of stock and bonds or on the rates of interest. If, for example, a corporation needs a large money supply in order to manufacture a new product, the investment bank arranges this. Their prime asset is their privileged position vis-à-vis financial information. "Some investment bankers maintain privately that the lifeblood of Wall Street is inside information."[14] In fact, they are primarily brokers in financial information. Investment banks have solidified their position with large corporate clients through representatives on the board of directors or via the holding of a considerable percentage of common stock. Figure 11 gives some of the directoral interlocks between investment banks and the information industry.

Investment bank Merrill Lynch has the world's largest chain of retail brokerage houses and is, together with Salomon Brothers, the key financial institution for Transamerica and since 1979 also for IBM.

Morgan Stanley has 24 of the 100 largest Fortune companies as its clients; among them are AT&T and General Electric.

Lehman Bros. manages funds for LTV and owns stock in the New York Times (2.19%), Burroughs (0.39%), Sperry Rand (0.38%), Singer 0.30%), ABC (0.28%), and RCA (0.24%). Lazard Frères, linked to S. Pearson, successfully managed funds for IT&T and EMI.

The investment banker, H. A. Allen holds a very significant interest in the film sector of the industry, with 25% of Columbia Pictures Industries. Presently Allen is involved in a fierce battle with the owner of another 25%, K. Kerkorian (who also holds 47% of MGM Film). As *Fortune* comments, Allen makes no bones about the stakes, "Columbia is in the best single business I want to be in for the next ten years."[15]

The New York based investment banks have over the years become the leaders for private placements, but also for mergers and acquisitions. The $1.5 billion merger of IT&T with Hartford Fire Insurance Co. in 1969, for example, was arranged by Lazard Frères. Recently, however, the large U.S. commercial banks have also started to move into this field more actively. Notable for its interest in the information industry is Bankers Trust Company of New York. One of the sections of its mergers and acquisitions group includes publishing and communications. This group has established

Bank \ Co	Grey	ABC	CPI	LTV	Pearson	Singer	Sperry Rand	20th Fox	Lockheed	Litton	COMSAT
Merrill Lynch	1								1		
Lazard Freres		1			1						
Drexel	1										
Allen	1		2								
Lehman				1				1		1	
INA						1	1				
Becker Warburg											1

Figure 11 Information Industry Interlocking Directorates with Investment Banks—1976

75

a computer data base that covers such categories as history of the property, circulation, advertising, readership and market position, management skills, corporate structure, and projection of future earnings.[16]

In general it can be said that an important goal of the management of a large industrial corporation will be corporate expansion. Among other benefits, the expansion is likely to increase the market value of the corporation's stock. An important way of securing large outside funds for expansion is borrowing from the banks. Borrowing also becomes a necessity for a corporation if it grapples with severe cash squeezes. An example is provided by Lockheed Aircraft in the 1970s. The company owed $400 million to a banking consortium led by Bankers Trust and Bank of America. In 1976 the banks converted the debt into $50 million equity and a $350 million term loan. They also lowered their interest rates. Lockheed obviously had to pay for this. As *Fortune* reported, "Part of the prize was an issue of ten-year warrants to purchase 3.5 million shares of common stock at what now look like bargain prices. If exercised, those warrants would give the banks a stunning 23.5 percent of Lockheed's equity. Since the warrants carried rights to buy at $7 and $10, and the stock has recently been around $18, the banks could realize an immediate profit of $30 million or more. Furthermore, in exchange for converting part of the debt to equity, the banks received 500,000 shares of $9.50 cumulative preferred shares. To date, dividends accrued on these shares total $4.5 million."[17]

Borrowing can be done through loans for shorter or longer periods, revolving credit agreements (the bank is committed to lend a certain amount for a specified rate of interest for longer than one year; the money can be used as the client needs it), or through lines of credit (this indicates the maximum fund a bank will lend to a client for a year). In cases where large scale funding is needed there are several banks involved. One among them is usually the lead supplier. This bank organizes the contribution of the other banks. It is obvious that the borrowing establishes a special relationship between bank and client, which can be corroborated through the banks' role in providing financial advice, information regarding possible mergers and acquisitions, and information about the credit position of the clients' customers.

INDUSTRIAL CONTROL

The question whether the described form of interdependence between banking and industry does constitute a form of control leads into a long standing and continuing debate on industrial control.

There is no need to record that debate here in all its details. It will suffice to highlight the major positions. In the present study the distinction between operational and allocative control is used. Operational control refers to the power to decisively influence the daily operations of a corporation. Allocative control refers to the power to decisively influence the allocation of corporate resources, the decisions about the corporate structure, expansion, long term product planning, and senior personnel appointments.

Allocative control is the focus of the present study, and the key question is which entity has more access than others to the execution of allocative control. This is a crucial question, particularly in an industrial branch that is strongly oligopolized and where market mechanisms do not balance out the goals and strategies of the corporate controllers. In such cases, allocative control decisively influences the market and, consequently, society at large. "The distribution of economic and political power, the predominant social values, the types of social and economic changes and reforms that are likely and possible—all of these are strongly influenced by the nature of control of large corporations."[18]

A very common position in the debate on control is known as the "managerial thesis," widely popularized by A. A. Berle and G. Means in the beginning of the 1930s.[19] The thesis claims that control has shifted from large stockholders, such as the banks, to a class of managers which, although owning a minor fraction of the shares, exercises the daily control and decides on all major issues.

This shift marks the separation of ownership from control. Supporting the thesis is the observation that since the 1930s stockholdings became widely dispersed and that the need for outside financing decreased, since growing profitability made internal funding possible.

The implication is greater power for corporate management and greater passivity for stockholders. As Berle and Means state, "In the corporate system, the 'owner' of industrial wealth is left with a mere symbol of ownership while the power, the responsibility and the substance which have been an integral part of ownership in the past are being transferred to a separate group in whose hands lies control."[20] Summing up the changes that affect the stockholders' position (such as no longer having the right to remove directors at will) Berle and Means conclude, "We have reached a condition in which the individual interest of the shareholder is definitely made subservient to the will of a controlling group of managers even though the capital of the enterprise is made up out of the aggregated contributions of perhaps many thousands of individuals."[21]

Berle and Means defined a corporation as management controlled in cases where no stockholder owned 5% of the stock and concluded that 44%

of the top 200 non-financial corporations in the U.S. were management controlled.

The books of a considerable number of economists have, since Berle and Means, elaborated the managerial thesis. Most noted among them are J. Burnham with *The Managerial Revolution* (in 1941), and J. K. Galbraith with *The New Industrial State* (in 1967). The thesis has been challenged by studies that provided empirical evidence for the continuing existence of owner control, or that proposed control by financial corporations. The latter proposition—financial control—is the most serious critique on the thesis of control by management. This is because the financial control thesis takes full account of the increasing importance of the institutional investors.

A first publication to point to this and to describe the alliance between institutional investors and management was J. A. Livingstone's *The American Stockholder* (in 1958).

In the 1950s millions of individuals in the U.S. bought stocks and bonds and the ownership of large corporations became widely dispersed.

At the end of 1956 institutional investors owned 24.5% of total stock outstanding. By the end of 1976 this had increased to 39.7%.[22] A similar development took place in the U.K. where, in 1963, institutional stockholders held 46% and, in 1975, 62.5% of the stock.[23]

In a projection for the U.S., R. M. Soldofsky expects that by the year 2000 institutional stockholdings will account for 55% of the market value of all outstanding stock.[24] Soldofsky concludes that among the institutional investors financial corporations are the most important, "the proportion of the market value of stock held by financial intermediaries has increased from about 13% in 1950 to about 25% by the end of 1968. Projections show a further increase to approximately 48% to 62% within about thirty years. When the overall market value ratio for financial intermediaries reaches this level, undoubtedly 50, 60, or 70% or even more of the voting stock of individual corporations is highly likely to be in the hands of financial intermediaries."[25] A similar development in the role of financial institutions is observable in the U.K. where, from 1963 to 1975, the stock held by them increased from 26.4% to 47.5%.

Concurrent with this observation goes the fact that many institutional investors devote increasing attention to the exercise of their voting rights. This results in more frequent challenges to management's decisions. Extra influence for the institutional investors is created because the rest of the stock is so dispersed and, in many cases, held by individuals and groups that do not particularly care about their voting rights.

D. J. Baum and N. B. Stiles in their study of institutional investors and corporate control conclude that there is a significant degree of influence, "(institutional investors) can strongly influence, if not ultimately determine, management action. They have the ability, the expertise to evaluate management intelligently. They have the financial resources which management seeks for its capital needs and which can be brought to bear, if necessary against management."[26]

The reference Baum and Stiles make to financial resources indicates that, contrary to the management thesis during the 1960s, it has become quite clear that large corporations continue to depend very much upon outside sources for their financing. This leads to the role of financial institutions.

Among the financial intermediaries, the banks are the most important institutional investors. In 1968 a U.S. House of Representatives Subcommittee issued a report on "Commercial Banks and Their Trust Activities" (the so-called Patman report, after the committee's chairman W. Patman).[27] The 49 banks surveyed by the study held 5% or more of the common stock in 147 out of the 500 largest industrial corporations in 1967. The Patman report concluded "the major banking institutions in this country are emerging as the single most important force in the economy."[28]

A number of U.S. government studies over the past years have corroborated this finding.[29]

A study by D. M. Kotz shows that by the late 1960s 34.5% of a sample from the 200 largest non-financial corporations were under financial control, i.e., financial institutions holding considerable power to influence fundamental corporate policies.[30] By the end of 1976 U.S. banks managed over 50% of all stock managed by institutional investors. Banks and their trust companies held half of the voting rights that institutional investors could exercise.[31] This key role of the banks also occurs in the Japanese economy, which is organized around strongly concentrated financial and industrial groups. "Group control in Japan stems basically from the heavy dependence on banks for finance, as Japanese companies rely on loans for up to 80% of capital, consequently the banks have considerable influence over companies, although by law they are restricted to a maximum 10% shareholding in a company."[32] The largest industrial groups are centered around the largest Japanese banks. The Dai Ichi Kangyo Bank (in 1976 the 2nd largest non-U.S. bank) is the nucleus of the DKB group (which includes Fujitsu). The Fuji Bank (in 1976 the 6th largest non-U.S. bank) is the nucleus of the Fuyo Group, and the Sumitomo Bank (in 1976 the 7th largest bank outside the U.S.) is one of the three leading companies in the Sumitomo Group (which includes NEC).

In France there are also strong links between banking and industry. Here a special point is that the French banks that are among the ten largest

non-U.S. banks are state-owned: Banque Nationale de Paris, Caisse Nationale de Crédit Agricole, and Crédit Lyonnais.*

In the Federal Republic of Germany there has recently been some un-
rest about the banks' control over industry. Early in 1979 the Minister of
Economics announced that he favored a drastic reduction in the banks' large
shareholdings in industry. The Minister proposed to limit a bank's holding
in a non-financial company to 15% of the stock. The German banks own
over 25% of the shares of many large industrial enterprises and provide the
majority of their credits.

In the U.K. the proportion of beneficial shareholdings by banks is
very low—in 1975 well under 1%. "As with British industry as a whole, the
banks are not major shareholders in communications corporations," concludes G. Murdock.[33] He adds to this, however, that links between the
industry and the merchant banks have become increasingly important.
Pearson & Son has direct links with Lazard Bros. & Co., the Rank Organization has direct links with Philip Hill and Investment Trust, and the Thomson Organization has direct links with Philip Hill, Investment Trust, S. G.
Warburg & Co., and the Hill Samuel Group.[34] In addition to the implications already mentioned, Murdock adds, "boardroom links with leading
concerns in other sectors play an important role in generating solidarity and
common consciousness among the various segments of monopoly capital."[35]

What then constitutes allocative control? Generally it is not possible
to find a single indicator for the measurement of industrial control. The
power to control is the function of the aggregate of a number of substantial
and relational attributes that an individual or institution may have access
to. These attributes can be divided into four categories and the more an
individual or institution has access to them the stronger the power to control will be.

Substantial attributes.   these include access to *capital supply* and to
common stock.

- Many large corporations need considerable outside funding and for
the most part they obtain this from a relatively small number of
transnational banks.[36] These banks can, in their function of creditors, exercise control. As D. M. Kotz remarks, "If the need for
funds is particularly urgent, for example, to move into a new, highly
attractive market, or, to replace obsolete facilities—then the likeli-

---

* State-owned banks account for 48% of French credits. The Mitterand administration has announced in July 1981 the nationalization of the largest private banks, such
as Banque de Paris et des Pays Bas, Cie Financière de SUEZ, and Crédit du Nord,
that account for some 25% of French credits.

hood of strong financial influence or control resulting is greater. The ultimate source of the power obtained by financial institutions in such situations is the threat of denying further funds, which could prevent the corporation from carrying out its plans."[37]

- The holding of common stock is "perhaps the single most important factor in determining control,"[38] as the Patman report suggested. The control implied here is in the right of the stockholder to vote and, potentially, to use this right against management. Moreover, as Kotz observes, "an institution can sell its holding suddenly, which would depress the price of the stock and hence harm the interests of management and other stockholders; or it could sell its holding to a group attempting to take over."[39] As different studies indicate, a holding of 5% of the common stock with voting rights by an institution or a homogeneous group of institutions already establishes an effective degree of control.

Relational attributes. these include access to influential networks created by *buyer-seller* links and *direct/indirect directoral links.*

- It is obvious that some degree of control is exercised by those institutions that are among the most important purchasers of the goods and services delivered by a corporation. Reference has been made to the case of the telecommunications industry, which sees its future growth and profitability as greatly dependent on such big customers as the banks.
- Directoral interlocks are created by a financial institution having a director on the board of a non-financial corporation. This is important because the board of the corporation is expected to make decisions on fundamental issues of corporate policy. Bankers are often on the boards of non-financial corporations as sources of financial advice and for contact with the financial community for eventual borrowing. Bankers can also represent the interests of their institutions as major debtholders or stockholders of the corporation. In the latter case, the degree of control is obviously greater.[40] A weaker link is formed by the indirect interlocks. Yet, if they are sufficiently numerous, they may constitute crucial avenues for the exchange of privileged information and important forums for joint decision-making. In any case they create great potential for anti-competitive abuse.[41]

The preceding discussion will now be applied to the transnational information industry.

CONCENTRATION OF STOCK

To study the question as to whether stockholdings are concentrated or dispersed in the information industry, the following index was used. Voting power by stockholders was considered concentrated in cases where:

1. one institutional investor controlled over 5% of the voting stock;
2. one individual or family group owned over 10%;
3. five or fewer institutional investors controlled over 10%.[42]

Analyzing the 62 information corporations for which stockholdings could be identified, concentration occurred in 77.5% of these corporations.

The distribution of the three categories was: 31% in (1); 29% in (2), and 14.5% in (3). Two corporations had concentrated stock ownership, but no specific category could be identified from the available data. They were Reed International (with 289 out of 71,415 shareholders owning 61.8% of the stock) and EMI (with 250 out of 62,059 shareholders owning 61% of the stock). If one were to apply the Berle and Means index for management control (occurring where no stockholder has over 5%), it could be concluded that 40% of the information industry corporations are management controlled. As we shall see later, in addition, in almost 15% of the corporations management has to share control to an important degree with larger financial institutions. Additionally, there are a number of cases where control could not readily be identified in which cases there is not necessarily a significant degree of management control. Thus a conservative estimate would lead to assuming that in some 20% of the information corporations there could be management control.

INSTITUTIONAL INVESTORS

Since the total number of stockholders could not be identified in all cases, it must be borne in mind that all the figures and percentages refer to data concerning identified stockholders.

Tables 36 and 37 give the proportions of voting stock held by institutional investors in U.S. and Japanese corporations. As the data collected for this study indicate, institutional investors own an average 34% of the voting stock of information corporations. Among the institutional investors, the banks hold 14.8%. These percentages are somewhat lower than the 1976 data for the U.S. total industry (39.7% institutional stockholdings, and half of them controlled by the banks). This is due to the fact, as we shall see later, that, especially, U.K. and German corporations have a strong individual/ family type ownership and the fact that, especially in the U.K. corporations, the banks are rather minimally represented.

Owner Control

A characteristic element of the information industry is the considerable number of cases in which one individual or one family group, often identical or strongly related to the original founder, has much of the voting stock. See Table 38.

Significant owner control exists in those corporations in which one individual or one family group holds over 10% of the voting stock, and no other stockholder owns a similar proportion. This type of control occurs in 24% of the corporations analysed. In 5% of the corporations, significant owner control was shared with a financial institution also owning a large proportion of the voting stock. In 3% of the cases, individuals had between 5% and 10% of the voting stock, and financial institutions had comparable percentages, while no other stockholders owned similar proportions.

Financial Control

In 8% of the corporations analyzed, significant owner control was shared with an equal degree of control by a bank or banking group.

Neither in the case of owner control nor in cases of financial control was a category of full control established in this study.[43] Full control seemed hardly a realistic concept. In practically all cases that were analyzed control was not exclusively in the hands of one individual or institution, but had to be shared to a greater or lesser degree with other parties. Therefore, two categories were established: a significant degree of financial control and a moderate degree of financial control. Indices for the degree of control were stockholdings, interlocking directorates, and debtholdings.[44] Data are in Figure 12 and Tables 39 through 46.

Significant financial control was applied to those cases in which:

- a corporation was a moderate-heavy borrower of funds; the lead supplier(s) was(were) represented on the board with one (or more) directors and/or owned voting stock (over 5% where stockholdings were concentrated and less where stockholdings were widely dispersed); either one combination was corroborated by: other banks owning jointly over 10% of the voting stock; and/or a banking group owning over 5% of the voting stock; and/or several banks having representatives on the board;

- one bank was the single largest stockholder with over 5% of the voting stock;
- one bank was the largest stockholder (and the stock was concentrated) and had a director on the board; or banks totalled over 10% of the voting stock and no other category of stockholders had a similarly large proportion; or banks were among the five top stockholders and had over 75% of their stock in cases of concentrated stockholdings; either one of these combinations was corroborated by several banks having representatives on the board of the corporation; or banks (banking groups) owning over 5% of the voting stock; or banks totalling over 10% of the voting stock with no other stockholders owning a similar proportion.

Moderate financial control was applied to those cases in which:

- a leading supplier of funds had a representative on the board and/or the corporation was a moderate to heavy borrower and this was corroborated by several indirect interlocking directorates or by banks totalling 5–10% of the voting stock;
- banks had less than 5% of the voting stock but still relatively large percentages as compared to other institutional investors and this was corroborated by representatives on the board and several indirect interlocking directorates;
- banks owned jointly less than 10% but were still the largest institutional stockholders and were lending to a moderate to heavy borrower;
- a bank had, in a situation of widely dispersed stock, a small percentage of the stock, but was the largest stockholder and banks jointly totalled between 5% and 10% of the voting stock.

Applying these criteria the distribution of information corporations according to the type of control is as follows (Table 47 gives the full information):

- Significant owner control: 24.1%
- Significant owner and significant financial control: 8.1%
- Significant financial control: 27.4%
- Moderate financial control: 14.5%

The remaining corporations (25.9%) fell into a miscellaneous category which comprised those cases in which a non-financial institutional investor owned over 10% of the voting stock or in which the center of control could not be identified.

Analyzing the data according to geographical patterns, the category of significant owner control occurs most frequently among corporations in the U.K. (62.5%) and the Federal Republic of Germany (50%). Significant financial control is most frequent among corporations in Japan (83%) and the U.S. (53%).

Combining the cases in which banks have the capacity to exert a significant degree of control, financial control occurs in 35.5% of the information corporations. Adding to this the cases in which banks are certainly among the influential allocative controllers, a significant to moderate degree of financial control is present in 50% of the information corporations. Out of the 8 corporations that constitute the nucleus of the transnational information industry (IBM, Philips, Siemens, EMI, General Electric, RCA, CBS, and MCA) 4 have a moderate to strong degree of financial control (IBM, Siemens, General Electric, and CBS).

In order to evaluate the significance of these data, they were compared with the results of the Kotz study. The comparison suffers, obviously, from the time difference between the two studies, but no other comparable sources could be found. Using those data that would fall into similar categories, Kotz found 39% of U.S. corporations under financial control. The present study found that 53% of U.S. information corporations was under financial control.

One could argue that the larger percentage of information corporations under financial control as compared to industry as a whole is due to the economic development in the years separating the two studies and simply reflects the increasing role of banks in controlling industry at large.

If one were, however, to take the category of significant financial control only, Kotz found that at the end of the 1960's 8% of the largest corporations he analyzed fell into this category. The present study finds that in the 1974–1977 period 24% of the U.S. information corporations fall in a similar category. This threefold increase seems very unlikely to reflect a general banking-industry relationship pattern. Moreover, already in Kotz' data there is a strong indication that banks are strongly linked with the information corporations in his sample and that the industrial sector that includes the manufacture of computers is 75% under financial control.[45]

Looking at the industrial sector, where financial control is strongest, the data indicate that the corporations that are under a significant degree of financial control are 22.7% involved with software and 77.3% with hardware (i.e., 36.3% dataprocessing + 32% telecommunications + 9% con-

Figure 12 Interlocks Between the 20 Largest *U.S. Commercial Banking Companies* (1976) and *U.S. Information Industries*

Banks \ Industries	ABC	AT&T	CBS	GE	GT&E	IBM	IT&T	RCA	Trans-Am	CDC	Honey-well	Inter-public	LTV
Bank of America Co.	1	4	2	1		5	1	1	1		1	1	
Citicorp.	1 / 4	1 / 18	1 / 10	1 / 11		3 / 10	3	1 / 8	5		1	1 / 2	1
Chase Manh. Co.	5	20	1	1 / 8		1 / 7	7	8			1 / 3		
Man. Hanover	1 / 5	2 / 17	12	1 / 3		11	8	5			3	3	1 / 1
J.P. Morgan	3	19	3	3 / 2		1 / 9	3	4			1	2	
Chemical N.Y.	4	2 / 10	15	1 / 7		2 / 17	5	6			2	2	1
Bankers Trust		1 / 17	1	11	1	1 / 12	1				1	1	
Cont. Illinois						1		1					
First Chicago	2	13	4	5		4		4	2		1 / 6	1	
Western Bancorp		1 / 3	2	2		1	2		2				
Sec. Pac. Corp.				1 / 3									
Wells Fargo			1	1 / 4		2	1		1				
Marine Midlands	4	4	4		1	5		1 / 1	2			1	
Crocker Nat. Corp.													
Charter N.Y. Corp.													
Mellon National		5		1	5	4		3					
First Nat. Boston	1	8				1		2	1		1	3	
Northwest Bancorp.		1						1		1	2 / 5		
First Bank System		2	1		1	1		1			2 / 8		
Nat. Detroit													

86

MCA	NCR	McG. Hill	N.Y. Times	Rock-well	Singer	Sperry	JWT	Time	20 Fox	TRW	Xerox	Dis-ney	Lock-heed	Litton	COM-SAT
1 /	1			7				2		1		1 / 3	1	1	
	2 /	3	2	1	2	1 / 4		5	1	5	1 / 4		3		6
	1	3	2		1	2 /		2		1	5		2		3
		4	2	3	1	2 / 1	2	3		2	5		4		1 /
	2	1 / 4	1		2	4		1		6	3		2		1 / 3
		3	4		5	8	1	2 / 4		2	8	1	1 / 4		1 / 6
	1	1 / 1	1 / 1		1	2		5			1 / 9		6	1	
1	1	1			1	1		3	1 /	4	1			1	
1 /					1	2		1 / 2	6	2			3	3	
1 /		2		1 / 9				1				2	1 / 3	1 /	
		2		1 /				2			1	2			
	1			2											
				2	1 /		1	2 /		1 /			1		
										1					
	1	1		1 / 1	1	3				2			2	2	1 / 3
											1				
1								1							
															1

Left upper is direct directoral links.

Right below is indirect directoral links.

One number only refers to indirect interlocks.

sumer electronics). This is a strong presence in the hardware branches, also given the fact that the software corporations constitute 47% of the total. This presence is further corroborated by the customer-supplier links that exist, particularly between the banks and the DP and telecommunications corporations.

Out of all software firms in the sample, 17% are to a significant degree controlled by the banks, of all hardware firms, 51% are controlled by the banks.

It could be argued that the considerable degree of financial control that is found in the information corporations is somewhat distorted by the fact that this is not always due to the influence of one particular bank, but to the combined strength of several banks. Indeed it would be an over simplification to consider the banking community as a closed, monolithic system with no competitive interests. This being true, it is also relevant to note that in many cases bankers have converging interests, that some banks have long standing alliances, and that the largest U.S. banks have considerable portions of each others' stock, and share many direct and indirect directoral interlocks. Long standing historical ties exist for example between Chase Manhattan and Chemical Bank (the Chase group), between Morgan Guaranty Trust and Bankers Trust (the Morgan group), and between Mellon Bank and the First National Bank of Boston. Already the Patman report found high levels of cross-ownership and self-control in the banking community. Cross-ownership is particularly strong among the major New York banks. The six largest New York banks (Citicorp., Chase Manhattan, Manufacturers Hanover, Morgan, Chemical and Bankers Trust) control almost 15% of the stock of Manufacturers Hanover, almost 10% of the stock of Citicorp, and almost 9% of Morgan. In all six cases the banks control over 5% of each other's stock. "Thus, these banks, which operate in the same domestic and foreign markets, have high financial stakes in each other and are potentially controlled or influenced by the same people they are supposedly competing with."[46]

Transnational banking is oligopolistically structured as was indicated in chapter 3. Transnational corporations tend to relate to a relatively few large transnational banks, usually domiciled in their home countries. Also, these banks are often strongly involved with the leading transnational corporations domiciled elsewhere. Taking significant control of a corporation in the home country plus a moderate degree of control vis-á-vis foreign corporations as an index, the banks and banking groups in Table 48 can be identified as the centers of financial control in the transnational information industry.

Significant relations refer to the holding of relatively important proportions of the voting stock, representation by directors on the board, and over 10 indirect interlocks. Involvement generally refers to leadership in lending to corporations, funds management, and/or minor proportions of voting stock.

SUMMARY

The data presented in this chapter indicate that there is a significant degree of financial control in the transnational information industry. This implies that particularly the banks have access to those substantial and relational attributes that constitute allocative control. There are especially strong linkages between the banks and the DP and telecommunications sectors of the information industry (representing 68% of the total sales of the industry).[47]

The converging areas of finance and information are oligopolistically controlled by the interlocking interests of a limited number of large transnational banks and large transnational information corporations.

NOTES TO CHAPTER 4

[1] *Telecommunications*, April 1980, p. 56.

[2] "The Film Council, A Brief History of the American Film Industry." In A. Mattelart and S. Siegelaub (eds), *Communication and Class Struggle*, International General, New York, 1979, Vol. I, p. 254.

[3] "The Film Council," op.cit., p. 259; P. Bächlin, *Ekonomiese Geschiedens van de Film*, Socialistische Uitgeverij, Nijmegen, 1977, p. 131.

[4] "The Film Council," op.cit., p. 256; P. Bächlin, op.cit., p. 131.

[5] "The Film Council," op.cit., p. 259.

[6] In 1980, the U.S. government curbed banks loans for the category that the Federal Reserve called "financing for speculative purposes." According to R. Kuhns, v.p., Bank of America's Entertainment Media Section, this would affect mainly small independent film companies. Kuhns commented in *Variety* (April 9, 1980) that Bank of America and other banks do not apply the Federal Reserve guidelines to the large entertainment companies but mostly to very small independents.

[7] A. Huet, J. Jon, A. Lefèbrve, B. Miège, and R. Peron, *Capitalisme et Industries Culturelles*, Presses Universitaires de Grenoble, Grenoble 1978, p. 164.

[8] *Variety*, Jan. 9, 1980, p. 97.

[9] A. Huet et al., op.cit., p. 164. In December 1980 the Banque de *Paris et des Pays Bas* increased its share in Hachette to 10%. The Banque Privée de Gestion Financière acquired 19%.

[10] J. Becker, "The Paper Crisis in Peripheral Capitalism," *Peace and the Sciences*, 1/1978, p. 14.

[11] Organisation for Economic Cooperation and Development, "Impact of Multinational Enterprises on National Scientific and Technical Capacities, Computer and Data Processing Industry," Paris 1977, p. 88.

[12] ibid., p. 59.

[13] *Business Week*, Oct. 1, 1979, p. 47.

[14] M. C. Jensen, *The Financiers*, Weybright and Talley, New York, 1976, p. 21.

[15] H. A. Allen in *Fortune*, Dec. 1, 1980, p. 67.

[16] *Editor & Publisher*, April 14, 1979, p. 16.

[17] *Fortune*, Oct. 1977, p. 203.

[18] D. M. Kotz, *Bank Control of Large Corporations in the United States*, University of California Press, Berkeley, 1978, p. 2.

[19] A. A. Berle and G. Means, *The Modern Corporation and Private Property*, Macmillan, New York, 1932.

[20] ibid., p. 68.

[21] ibid., p. 227-278.

[22] "Voting Rights in Major Corporations," a staff study prepared by the Subcommittee on Reports, Accounting, and Management of the U.S. Senate Committee on Governmental Affairs, Washington, 1978, p. 594.

[23] G. Murdock, "Mass Media and the Class Structure," Report, Centre for Mass Communication Research, University of Leicester, June 1979, p. 17.

[24] R. M. Soldofsky, *Institutional Holdings of Common Stock, 1900-2000*, Bureau of Business Research, University of Michigan, Ann Arbor, 1971, p. 209.

[25] ibid., p. 105.

[26] D. J. Baum and N. B. Stiles. *The Silent Partners: Institutional Investors and Corporate Control*, Syracuse University Press, Syracuse, 1965, p. 159.

[27] "Commercial Banks and Their Trust Activities: Emerging Influence on the American Economy," by the Subcommittee on Domestic Finance of the U.S. House of Representatives' Banking and Currency Committee, Washington, 1968.

[28] ibid., p. 5.

[29] See i.a., "Institutional Investor's Common Stock," by the Subcommittee on Reports, Accounting, and Management of the U.S. Senate Committee on Government Operations, May 1976:

"Interlocking Directorates among the Major U.S. Corporations," by the Subcommittee on Reports, Accounting, and Management of the U.S. Senate Committee on Government Affairs, January 1978;

"Voting Rights in Major Corporations," by the Subcommittee on Reports, Accounting, and Management of the U.S. Senate Committee on Governmental Affairs, Jan. 1978.

[30] D. M. Kotz, op.cit., p. 97.

[31] Data from the *Institutional Investor*, August 1977.

[32] Dodwell Marketing Consultants, *Industrial Groupings in Japan*, rev. ed., 1978, p. i.

[33] G. Murdock, op.cit., p. 18.

[34] ibid., Table 13.

[35] ibid., p. 21.

[36] R. B. Cohen, "Lending by Transnational Banks and Other Financial Institutions to Transnational Corporations," Report to the United Nations Centre on Transnational Corporations, New York, 1979.

[37] D. M. Kotz, op.cit., p. 21.

[38] "Commercial Banks and Their Trust Activities: Emerging Influence on the American Economy," op.cit., p. 23.

[39] D. M. Kotz, op.cit., p. 19.

[40] Regarding interlocking directorates, a 1951 study by the U.S. Federal Trade Commission notes, "Interlocking relations between manufacturing corporations and financial institutions, especially banks and insurance companies, may establish a type of vertical relation that assures adequate credit to favored companies and a withholding of credit and capital from their competitors," pp. 21, 23.

[41] "Potentials for Abuse," in "Interlocking Directorates among the Major U.S. Corporations, op.cit., pp. 3-9.

[42] "Voting Rights in Major Corporations," op.cit., p. (1).

[43] The category "full financial control" was used in the study by D. M. Kotz, op.cit.

[44] Sources for *stockownership* include:
G. Murdock, "Mass Media and the Class Structure," Report, Centre for Mass Communication Research, University of Leicester, June 1979. Dodwell Marketing Consultants, *Industrial Groupings in Japan*, rev. ed., 1978.
Corporate Data Exchange, New York, 1979—a sample of the stock profiles prepared for the present study by CDE can be found in Appendix III.
"Institutional Investors' Common Stock," Study prepared for the Subcommitte on Reports, Accounting, and Management of the U.S. Senate Committee on Government Operations, May 1976.
"Voting Rights in Major Corporations," Study prepared for the Subcommittee on Reports, Accounting, and Management of the U.S. Senate Committee on Governmental Affairs, Jan. 1978.
DAFSA, Paris, 1977.
Wer gehört zu wem, Commerzbank, 1979.
Annual reports from corporations and banks.
Sources for *interlocking directorates* include:
"Interlocking Directorates among the Major U.S. Corporations," Study prepared by the Subcommittee on Reports, Accounting, and Management of the U.S. Senate Committee on Governmental Affairs, Jan. 1978.
Proxy statements for annual meetings of stockholders with U.S. corporations in 1976 and 1977.
Standard & Poor's *Register* of Directors and Executives.
G. Murdock, op.cit.
Annual reports from corporations and banks.
Sources for *debt holdings* include:

R. B. Cohen, "Lending by Transnational Banks and Other Financial Institutions to Transnational Corporations," Report to the United Nations Centre on Transnational Corporations, 1979.

Dodwell Marketing Consultants, op.cit.

D. M. Kotz, op.cit.

Annual reports from corporations and banks.

The data collected for this study cover the 1974-1977 period.

[45] D. M. Kotz, op.cit., passim and p. 193.

[46] CDE Handbook, op.cit., p. 13.

[47] A study by the U.S. Senate Committee on Governmental Affairs ("Structure of Corporate Concentration," published 1980) corroborates the finding of strong inter-locks between financial institutions and the DP and telecommunications sectors.

5

Conclusions

The material offered in the preceding chapters suggests the existence of a highly oligopolised transnational information industry with strong financial needs and interests and the existence of a highly oligopolised transnational banking system with strong informational needs and interests.

It also suggests the increasing convergence of interests between information corporations and the banks. This has a number of aspects.

1. There is a convergence due to developments which integrate computer and telecommunications technologies into the digital transfer of all kinds of information. All information flows become digital data flows. Money traffic becomes digital bits traffic. Distinctions between traditionally separated types of information flows become obsolete.
2. There is an operational convergence in which information corporations become involved in the trading of financial information and actual banking services and banks become involved in a variety of informational services.
3. There is a financial interdependence in which information corporations need large scale funding and banks are credit suppliers. Creditor-debtor relations are corroborated by stock ownership of the banking system in the information industry and representation

on its boards of directors, thus leading to strong coalescing interests between few information corporations and few banks.

As the present study has shown, the transnational information industry is
characterized by a relatively strong degree of financial control. Thus the
banks potentially have the capacity to decisively influence corporate policy
on a wide scale of fundamental issues.

This amounts to a convergence of interests between two key institutions in advanced capitalism. By key institutions are meant those social
actors that have the power to influence crucial decisions in society. This
power is based upon their capacity to mobilize fundamental resources for
such decisions. This capacity is dependent upon the access to those infrastructures that make it possible to influence decisively the allocation of
resources.

There can be little doubt that in advanced capitalism, money is a
fundamental resource. Crucial, however, is the control of its allocation:
"the power to decide who gets money and who doesn't is a critical force in
our society."[1] The large transnational banks, controlling the allocation of
vast amounts of money, operating in a multitude of financial markets, and
performing a great variety of financial services have a great capacity to
mobilize this resource for decisions according to their interests.

Similarly, information is a fundamental resource. With advanced
capitalism shifting the focus of its economic activity increasingly towards
the processing and distributing of information, this is even more so. The
transnational information industry has access to the infrastructures for the
processing and distributing of this resource and thus has the capacity to
mobilize it for decisions in accordance with its interests!

The question for this last chapter then is: which are the implications of
the convergence of interests between the transnational information industry
and the transnational banking system? Four levels on which implications
could have far-reaching ramifications need to be discussed.

MONEY TRANSFER AS DATA TRANSFER:
BANKING AND TRANSBORDER DATA FLOWS

Huge masses of data flow across the globe: In different formats—as
raw data, machine-readable data, or computerized information; via different signals—analogous or digital; through different media—post, telex, telephone, data networks. Most of the data continue to be transported in rather

traditional ways. This pertains also to banking transmissions. Increasingly, however, as was indicated in the preceding chapter, computerized data networks are created that carry, rapidly and reliably, enormous quantities of information in the form of digital signals. Since financial data account, most probably, for a significant portion of these signals, the question is raised on how banking interests will affect transborder data flows. A tentative answer points to the following:

1. Transnational banks will consider it crucial for their managements' decision making on a global scale to have centralized access to vital information on all the banking activities carried out with their customers. Therefore, centralized dataprocessing will be a key requirement. The consequence is, as R. E. I. Walker of Continental Illinois National Bank comments, "The inhibition or restriction in any way of data flow from one unit to the head office would degrade the whole concept of this centralized processing system."[2] The general feeling within the banking system is that restrictive legislation on transborder data flow would seriously hinder the banks' operations: "erode centralized decision-making, hamper global management, and curtail the creation of new financial services."[3] Evidently then, transnational banks will militate very strongly against any restraint imposed on what they conceive of as a free flow of information and will favor a largely deregulated information industry.[4] This means that in the present international political debate, (i.a., in the UNESCO fora) the Western information media have found some rather powerful allies in their efforts to protect free flow interests. The technological convergence gives the bankers-media connection an extra impetus, as Citibank vice president W. Sparks explains. "Since the digital information flowing in cables or moving through space will be, in effect, a single, homogeneous stream, it will become increasingly impossible to maintain any of the traditional distinctions between transmissions carrying news, entertainment, financial data, or even personal phone calls. This intermixing of data will make it impossible to pass laws restricting the transmission of one kind of information without impinging on all the others. Efforts to impede the flow of capital must inevitably lead to restrictions imposed on the flow of information, and vice versa."[5]

2. Transnational banks will need standardization of systems in the different units for their centralized processing. As Citibanks' R. B. White states, "We would encourage any international effort that would eliminate barriers and increase flexibility in selecting tele-

communication equipment and transmission technologies."[6] White is less certain than Walker in the need for standardized equipment, but he would at least want to see compatible equipment. Adding this to the need for the utilization of large scale sophisticated equipment, this implicitly supports the continued worldwide dependence on the few leading computer and telecommunications manufacturers.

3. Transnational banks will want to transmit huge volumes of data over great distances. They will tend to turn away from those public carriers that charge volume-sensitive and distance-sensitive tariffs and will rather use leased private circuits with better economies.

4. "Confidentiality is a cornerstone of banking throughout the world" (R. B. White). Banks will for privacy and for economic reasons want to keep their data flows protected from any inspection. Technically this is quite possible. Random routing through different parts of the network, direct transmission via satellites, or encryption make any form of border control on transborder data flows futile. Here a complex problem arises. Certain national governments do not allow the transmission of encrypted messages. In several European countries this is considered an important national security rule.[7] At the same time, however, it reduces the privacy of what is transmitted through the data flows. Banks, however, do not transmit only personal data but also financial information that a country may rightly find damaging to its national economic security if it leaves the country.

5. The fact that banks become increasingly involved with computer communications also has effects on the banks themselves. Electronic funds transfers, computerized tellers, and automated administrative procedures will have significant influence on the employment in the banking sector. The Nora/Minc report projects that the installation of new computer systems could lead the banks to need 30% less personnel in the next 10 years.[8] Moreover, the "informatization" of the banks will create new forms of electronic embezzlement and will demand new ways of credit authorization. All this will have far-reaching social implications.

6. Another aspect of transborder data flows affecting the banking system is the increased money velocity. The computer-communication networks will drastically increase the speed at which money (=information) changes hands in society and on a global scale. Will this lead to a rapid growth of expenditures, will it act as an increase in money supply that by far exceeds the available goods and

services for purchase? Will this contribute to worldwide inflation?[9] Or will, as S. Rose argues, the electronic transfer of funds (EFT) help to curtail inflation? According to Rose, EFT will contribute to the raising of savings and will free up a considerable amount of human and other resources now locked up in an oversized and inefficient financial industry. He expects, through a redeployment of these resources in sectors of the economy where they can be more profitably used, a rising national output and an increase in the supply of goods and services which will hold down the price level.[10] Another aspect of the increased rapidity of money transfer is the fact that the time-margin between the order of a funds transfer and the receiving of funds disappears. How will the interim-interests that used to be important for the banks now be compensated for? For which services will the customers' price be increased?

7. The implication of the statement quoted from S. Rose is that EFT will strongly contribute to the concentration of the banking system. EFT will lead to a situation where fewer banks hold the major portion of society's financial assets. An important factor here is the capital intensity of the necessary technological infrastructure. Technology for data communications is very expensive, and involvement in EFT demands considerable increases in a bank's "up-front" investments. "A funds transfer system, requiring more sophisticated terminals and interbank switches, would command at least $1 million of hardware expense, create greater management problems, and cause vastly expanded systems support expense."[11] Additionally, it may well be that after five years the maintenance expense will become even greater than the equipment expense. The application of advanced information technology will strengthen the trend towards oligopolistic control of the banking system. The largest banks will be the first to install the most sophisticated machinery, and this will seriously affect the capacity of smaller banks to compete.

8. Transborder data flows also imply increasing chances to escape governmental control on the international flow of capital. It has always been very difficult for government to control capital flows, but the advanced information technology fundamentally challenges the national sovereign powers. A good example is provided by the Euromarket: the pool of stateless cash that finds its origin in the 1950s and 1960s when the governments of the U.K. and the U.S. tried to restrict the role of their national currencies in international trade transactions and placed ceilings on rates of interests in sup-

port of their domestic economies. The money supply simply shifted from national markets to a newly created uncontrolled Euromarket. As a *Time* commentary describes this market. "Supermoney is the immense and swift moving pool of currencies deposited in banks outside their home-countries—and thus out of the control of any government."[12] The estimated $1 trillion dollar-pool has created a new source of investment capital and has certainly contributed to more international trade. For commercial bankers the Eurocurrency market supplies crucial investment funds for transnational corporations and provides the mechanism through which OPEC countries can trade their petrodollars. For most governments the Euromarket is, as Italy's former central banker, G. Carli, describes it, "the root of all evil in the international monetary system."[13] It is seen to contribute largely to financial instability and to disrupt national attempts at curbing inflation. Information technologies play an important role. The possibility of trading currencies practically instantaneously creates monetary instability and can easily drive down a currency's value.

Most of the Euromarket transactions occur electronically, and this is a major reason for the diminishing potential of governments to control them. "Private bankers warn that attempts to regulate will fail."[14] As Citibank's vice president, W. Sparks, concludes, "The Euromarket is a paradigm of what happens when governments attempt to control the flow of capital in the new era of international communications."[15] The application of modern information technology has greatly increased the power of the transnational banks vis-à-vis the power of national governments.

FINANCIAL INFORMATION:
THE NEW INTERNATIONAL ECONOMIC ORDER AND
THE NEW INTERNATIONAL INFORMATION ORDER

The increased power of the transnational banks to escape national legislation evidently affects the national governments of less developed countries most drastically.

Financial information flows across the globe in the form of computer data through the banking networks and in the form of economic news through transnational newsagencies and newspapers. Financial data—an important segment of overall transborder data flows—is controlled by the large transnational banks that own and/or operate transnational computer-communication systems. Also, they have privileged access to vital financial information through more traditional means.

Financial data base services controlled by Chase Econometrics, Reuters, and the AP-Dow Jones combination supply most of the world's demand for financial information. Financial information to the business community at large is accounted for primarily by the 7 leading financial newspapers: the *Financial Times* (U.K.), the *Wall Street Journal* (U.S.A.), the *Australian Financial Review*, the *Gazeta Mercantil* (Brazil), the *Handelsblatt* (FRG), *Il Sole-24 Ore* (Italy), and the *Nihon Keizai Shimbun* (Japan).

Financial information flows follow the general pattern of international communications. There is a two-way traffic among the countries of the North and between those countries and the countries of the South. The nature of the traffic differs with its direction. From the South flow, primarily, "raw" materials (data in unprocessed form), and the reversed flow contains primarily ready-made information packages. In the North the U.S. transmits processed information to Western Europe and Japan and receives, to a lesser degree, similar packages. Western Europe sends large volumes of data for processing to the U.S.

In a very unfortunate move, recent political gatherings (particularly the 20th UNESCO General Conference in 1978) have moved away from the concept of "a new international information order." A more acceptable formulation was found with "a more effective and more just world communication and information order." This is unfortunate because it tends to obscure the indissoluble link between the demand for a restructuring of informational relations between nations and the demand to establish a new international economic order.[16]

With even more countries (also the newly industrializing countries) moving rapidly towards becoming information economies, with information goods and services taking a crucial place in world trade, and with the information-industrial complex comprising the largest transnational corporations, with industrial corporations calculating a major portion of their production costs as information costs, *information* and *economy* are integrally bound together.

This is strongly underlined by the present evidence on the close relations between the banking system and the information-industry. There is a strong mutual dependency and close interlocking. A decisive consequence of this is the fact that the access to such an essential resource as financial information is oligopolistically controlled by the "financial-information-industrial complex."

Access to the whole range of financial information is the privileged property of few private enterprises in the North. It needs only a little imagination to see the disadvantages this implies for the countries of the South.

The present differential access to financial/economic information is an important determinant in the deployment of the world's resources. Take the example of the oil price increase by the OPEC countries in 1973. "Telecommunication networks between the major central banks helped Japan, West Germany, France, the U.K., and the U.S. forecast their oil import bills and formulate policies to combat the ensuing internal inflation."[17]

A particularly pertinent case in point is related to the expanding private international lending. Large transnational banks began to play a crucial role in lending to Third World countries in 1972. By 1976 an estimated 40% of the total Third World debt was owed to private sources. This was about $75 billion, of which $45 billion was owed to U.S. banks.[18] The essential question for Third World countries, vis-à-vis this private circuit, is how they acquire information about all the complex and swiftly changing aspects of the international financial system. How do they know sufficiently early and reliably about rates of exchange or rates of interest? This would demand access to the international financial information brokerage circuit, but also to the vast and expensive systems for the processing and distributing of the information.

The quest for a new international order will have to choose as one of its focal points the access to financial information.

Here the convergence of economic and informational structures becomes most transparent. At this crossroad the strongest interests are invested, the problems are most acute and—at the same time—rapid technological developments make chances for their solution increasingly slim.

OLIGOPOLY ON THE
INFORMATION TECHNOLOGY MARKET

As several U.S. Senate studies have stated, the interlocks between financial institutions and users of financial services create great potential for anti-trust abuse. Such vertical interlocks tend to disrupt free markets, distort competition, and injure the interests of smaller producers and consumers. They also make corporations that are supposed to compete in an industrial sector into allies that are strongly inclined to favor cooperation in price setting. "As a vertical interlock between borrowers and lenders, the institutional interlock, when multiplied, may lead to indirect horizontal interlocks between competitors."[19]

Moreover, as Kotz argues, "financial control may affect the behaviour of firms not only toward competitors, but also toward potential customers or suppliers."[20] Financial control contributes to the formation of strong links between certain suppliers and certain customers, thus strengthening the concentration of the market. Particularly in the case of the banking-system/ information industry interlock, there are important supplier-customer converging interests. Information technology—both as equipment and services—is mainly designed for large customers, among which the banks play an increasingly important role. Financial control plus these vertical supplier-customer interlocks create a strong degree of concentration on the information technology market. Its functioning tends to become determined by the converging interests of few producers and few customers. The needs of the small individual consumers tends to be met by the so-called "spin-offs" which, with skillful "management of demand" (Galbraith), are sold as if they were produced for them in the first place. On the information technology market there is no place for small or medium-sized independent producers. Thus the avowed principle of the market economy that there should be free competition is violated.

BANKS AND THE VISIBLE INFORMATION FLOWS

The present study has not concentrated on the issue of banks and mass media interlocks. The data collected showed the strongest interlocks between the banking system and the hardware sectors of the information industry. The focal point thus became the so-called "invisible information flows." Yet, the visible counterpart, the information through the world's mass media has not escaped the bankers' interests. As investment banker H. Allen declares about the film industry: "selling software is even better than the oil business."[21] As the data show, the banking system is also involved in those corporations that sell information as a commodity. This can be very profitable and—logically—where banks are present their main interest is the profit maximization of the firms they relate to. The fact that they as stockholders (beneficiary or not) and/or creditors are primarily pursuing policies that lead to maximum profits implies that their foremost interest is with the exchange-value of the commodity the corporation produces/distributes. It is important to observe that it is inherent in the contradictions of the capitalist economy, that high exchange-values do not exclude ideological use values contrary to the interests of the financiers.[22] Information is an attractive investment object. As M. U. Porat explains, "information does not even depreciate with use. . . . the more one uses certain types of information, the more valuable they become."[23] The emphasis here has to be on the qualification "certain types," because it is also true, as E. McAnany states, that information "can lose its economic value when it becomes widely available."[24] Information is financially attractive in the form of privileged propietary data with restricted circulation and, through this, with an economic value attached to it.

Information is also financially attractive in the form of public information, with a value that increases the more one can sell of it.

With regard to the latter, the question here is will the interlocks between the media-producers and the banks have implications for their production and distribution.

1. This will indeed be the case, because of the capital intensity of information supply and distribution. Privileged customer-capital supplier relationships restrict the number of information suppliers and distributors.

2. "The phenomenon of financial control has created a much higher degree of concentration of power than would exist in its absence."[25] Close interlocks with the banking system may not include direct influence on the information production process; they certainly lead to the selective strengthening of certain producers over against others. Thus, the closer the interlocks with the banking system the greater the industrial concentration.

3. On a supposedly free information market, the contents of media ought to be pluriform and autonomous. The question is, however, do the media corporations sufficiently represent the broad variety of society's actors and are they sufficiently autonomous from other powerful segments of the society?[26] The close interlocks with such a powerful segment of society as the banking system makes this highly debatable. Are the media capable of criticising the power elites and society's differential access to its basic resources, or do the interlocks limit their role to maintaining and legitimising social inequality? As a *Columbia Journalism Review* study on interlocking directorates suggests, "For despite the financial benefits that accrue to newspaper companies with bankers and former government officials on their boards, the fact remains that such ties may have adverse journalistic consequences. Some of these may be subtle-unconscious self-censorship, for example. In other cases the consequences have been manifest-reporters pressured, stories unassigned or killed when written. The concern with interlock, therefore, reaches beyond traditional worries about antitrust. The concern centers on the flow of information and vitality of journal-

ism as something absolutely disinterested and relentlessly independent."[27]

ALLOCATIVE CONTROLLERS

Finance and information are converging areas. Their industrial representatives (the banks and the information industry) have strong converging interests. At the heart of the convergence, a limited number of large transnational banks have access to the capacitating structure that enables them to decisively influence the allocation of the resource information. This capacitating structure may not necessarily be utilized at all times, but its presence implies that fundamental allocative control in society is potentially in the hands of few social actors only. This seriously collides with those proposals, put forward by Third World countries in particular, that project a democratic and participatory exchange of information to which all social actors contribute.

The convergence of interests between finance and information is not an incidental and passing phenomenon. It is rather an inherent characteristic of the present international information and economic order. Its only real remedy is a fundamental restructuring of that order.

Short of implementing such far reaching measures, the present situation demands, at least minimally, that the distribution and execution of control in society be exposed. "The hands on the levers of control of giant corporations must be visible to the public, for its own protection," as a U.S. Senate study recommends.[28] Because, to quote I. Gadourek, "Silencing power relations is the safest technique to retain power."[29]

NOTES TO CHAPTER 5

[1] CDE Handbook, *Banking and Finance*, New York, 1980, p. 7.

[2] Testimony R. E. L. Walker before the Subcommittee on Government. Information and Individual Rights of the U.S. House of Representatives Committee on Government Operations, Washington, March 1980.

[3] ibid.

[4] In this context it is interesting to note that at the Bank Telecommunications '80 (the 4th annual American Bankers Association workshop), U.S. Congressman L. Van Deerlin and Senator D. Riegle strongly advised the banking community to support the revisions of the 1934 Communications Act that sought to deregulate the information industry.

[5] W. Sparks, "The Flow of Information and the New Technology of Money," Address at the Conference on World Communications: Decisions for the Eighties, at the Annenberg School of Communications, Philadelphia, May 1980, p. 7.

[6] Testimony of R. B. White in Hearings before the Subcommittee on International Operations of the U.S. Senate Committee on Foreign Relations, Washington, June 1977.

[7] J. Freese, *International Data Flow*, Studentlitteratur AB, Lund, 1979, p. 52.

[8] S. Nora and A. Minc, *L'Informatisation de la Société*, La Documentation Francaise, Paris, 1978, p. 36.

[9] A. Toffler, *The Eco-Spasm Report*, Bantam Books, New York, 1975, p. 33.

[10] S. Rose, "The Unexpected Fall Out from Electronic Banking," *Fortune*, April 24, 1978.

[11] J. B. Benton, "Electronic Funds Transfer: Pitfalls and Payoffs," *Harvard Business Review*, July-Aug. 1977, pp. 20-22.

[12] *Time*, Nov. 5, 1979, p. 60.

[13] ibid.

[14] ibid.

[15] W. Sparks, op. cit., p. 3.

[16] For a further discussion of this topic, see C. J. Hamelink (ed), *Communication in the Eighties, a Reader on the McBride Report*, IDOC, Rome, 1980, pp. 50-52.

[17] M. Jussawalla, *Development Communication Report*, July 1978.

[18] H. M. Wachtel, *The New Gnomes: Multinational Banks in the Third World*, Transnational Institute, Washington, 1977, p. 11.

[19] Quote from former Federal Trade Commission chairman L. Engman in "Interlocking Directorates among the Major U.S. Corporations," a Study prepared by the Subcommittee on Reports, Accounting, and Management of the U.S. Senate Committee on Governmental Affairs, Washington, 1978, p. 7.

[20] D. M. Kotz, *Bank Control of Large Corporations in the United States*, University of California Press, Berkeley, 1978, p. 135.

[21] H. Allen in *Fortune*, December 1, 1980.

[22] Thus films and books can be brought on the market that may take issue with their corporate producers/distributors as long as they are profitably sold.

[23] M. U. Porat, "Global Implications of the Information Society," *Journal of Communication*, Winter 1978, p. 79.

[24] E. McAnany, "Does Information Really Work?" *Journal of Communication*, Winter 1978, p. 85.

[25] D. M. Kotz, op. cit., p. 145.

[26] M. Clement, *The Canadian Corporate Elite*, McClelland and Stewart, Toronto, 1975, p. 283.

[27] P. Dreier and S. Weinberg, "Interlocking Directorates, Newspaper Companies, and the Institutions They Cover," *Columbia Journalism Review*, Nov.-Dec. 1979, p. 53.

[28] "Voting Rights in Major Corporations," a Study by the Subcommittee on Reports, Accounting, and Management of the U.S. Senate Committee on Governmental Affairs, Washington, 1978, p. 4.

[29] I. Gadourek, quoted in H. M. Helmers et al., *Graven naar Macht*, Van Gennep, Amsterdam, 1975, p. 43.

Tables

Table 1
Information Industry Sales (1976)[1]

Rank	Corporation	Sales in Thousands	% Info. Goods/ Services	Total Employees	Country
1	AT&T[2]	32,815,582	100	927,200	U.S.
2	IBM	16,304,333	100	291,977	U.S.
3	Philips	5,991,205 (est)	52	391,500	H.
4	GT&E[2]	5,746,262	85	194,000	U.S.
5	Matsushita	5,422,644	62.6	83,081	J.
6	RCA	4,584,000	85.5	110,000	U.S.
7	Xerox	4,403,897	100	97,336	U.S.
8	IT&T	4,117,437 (est)	35	375,000	U.S.
9	International Paper	3,540,600	100	52,287	U.S.
10	General Electric	3,453,406 (est)	22	380,000	U.S.
11	Siemens	2,982,352 (est)	37	304,000	F.R.G.
12	AEG/Telefunken	2,675,694 (est)	50	161,900	F.R.G.
13	Hitachi	2,605,364 (est)	39	143,014	J.
14	Reed International	2,580,841	100	86,300	U.K.
15	Sperry Rand	2,025,900	63.2	87,090	U.S.
16	CBS	1,980,900	88.8	30,500	U.S.
17	Rockwell	1,966,000	37.7	119,117	U.S.
18	Thomson-Brandt	1,908,120 (est)	54	105,600	F.R.
19	NCR	1,906,998	72.4	67,000	U.S.
20	Burroughs	1,870,845	87	49,884	U.S.
21	Nippon Electric	1,608,577	89	56,258	J.
22	Sony	1,505,122	100	22,713	J.
23	Rank Xerox	1,418,850	100	30,313	U.K./U.S.
24	Control Data	1,358,259	67	33,961	U.S.
25	Honeywell	1,342,000	53,8	70,775	U.S.
26	ABC	1,306,266	97	9,000	U.S.
27	Ericsson	1,304,483	74	71,100	S.W.
28	EMI	1,224,102 (est)	84	51,300	U.K.
29	Lockheed	1,210,000	37.7	54,600	U.S.
30	Fujitsu	1,171,318	100	31,693	J.
31	Litton	1,129,054	33.5	92,800	U.S.
32	Northern Telecom	1,127,966	100	25,277	C.D.
33	Olivetti	1,125,891	82.6	68,997	I.T.
34	TRW	1,049,000	35	87,625	U.S.
35	Grundig	1,017,183	100	34,570	F.R.G.
36	Plessey	991,862	100	63,890	U.K.
37	Hachette	990,873	100	5,683	F.R.
38	CGE	863,476	26.3	130,200	F.R.
39	Bertelsmann	842,520	100	21,829	F.R.G.
40	Warner Communications	791,228	95.7	6,200	U.S.
41	Time Inc.	741,700	71.4	12,500	U.S.
42	Digital Equipment	736,288	100	25,000	U.S.
43	Polygram	714,286	100	12,800	F.R.G./H.
44	MCA	685,683	85.4	14,000	U.S.
45	Texas Instruments (1977)	677,000	39.2	66,162	U.S.
46	Bosch	661.156	20	110.800	FRG
47	CII-Honeywell Bull	658,048	100	18,752	F.R.
48	Gulf & Western	645,400	15	110,000	U.S.
49	McDonnell Douglas	593,000	16.7	57,867	U.S.
50	ICL	548,757	100	27,317	U.K.
51	McGraw Hill	546,256	92.6	11,466	U.S.

Table 1 (continued)

Rank	Corporation	Sales in Thousands	% Info. Goods/ Services	Total Employees	Country
52	Sanyo	530,528	100	8,120	J.
53	LTV	502,500	11.2	56,800	U.S.
54	New York Times	451,425	100	6,700	U.S.
55	Toshiba	445,993	10	105,000	J.
56	Singer	418,900	19.8	85,000	U.S.
57	Rank Organization	415,232	61.3	38,201	U.K.
58	Nixdorf	384,000	100	10,000	F.R.G.
59	Transamerica	377,711	14	25,800	U.S.
60	Washington Post	375,729	100	4,700	U.S.
61	20th Century Fox	351,474	100	5,200	U.S.
62	Decca	325,292	100	12,064	U.K.
63	Columbia Pictures	318,100	81.5	2,800	U.S.
64	Thomson Organization	297,995	58	22,674	U.K.
65	News International	251,292	100	9,157	U.K.
66	S. Pearson	231,824	44.3	30,000	U.K.
67	Nielsen	231,652	100	12,966	U.S.
68	J.W. Thompson	161,476	100	5,350	
69	Disney Productions	160,139	27.4	16,000	U.S.
70	COMSAT	153,649	100	1,355	U.S.
71	Young & Rubicam	139,848	100	3,980	U.S.
72	McCann Erickson	133,551	100	4,827	U.S.
73	MGM	123,315	45	6,000	U.S.
74	Ogilvy & Mather	122,226	100	4,600	U.S.
75	ATV/ACC	122,207	76.3	5,023	U.K.
76	Playboy	108,211	54.7	3,740	U.S.
77	Burnett	106,301	100	2,900	U.S.
78	Associated Press	100,000	100	2,500	U.S.
79	BBDO	96,400	100	2,121	U.S.
80	SSC&B	96,000	100	2,730	U.S.
81	Bates	93,488	100	2,939	U.S.
82	Reuters	80,000	100	1,035	U.K.
83	UPI (1977)	73,000	100	1,326	U.S.
84	D'Arcy McManus	71,985	100	2,200	U.S.
85	Foote & Cone	68,216	100	2,293	U.S.
86	AFP	43,000	100	1,985	F.R.

Total Sales: $147,430,643,000
Total Employees: 6,000,400

Key for Country Abbreviations

U.S.	United States of America
U.K.	United Kingdom
H.	Holland
J.	Japan
F.R.G.	Federal Republic of Germany
F.R.	France
I.T.	Italy
S.W.	Sweden
C.D.	Canada

[1] Figures in this table are calculated from various sources, i.e., *Fortune, Datamation, Advertising Age,* corporations' annual reports and (for US firms) 10 K forms.

[2] For AT&T and GT&E these figures refer to operating revenues. The employees' figure for AT&T includes its wholly owned subsidiary Western Electric.

Table 2
Sectors of the Information Industry

Sectors	Goods/Services
1. Data Processing	Mainframe computers Mini computers Peripheral equipment Software and services Databases and databanks
2. Telecommunication	*Equipment:* telephone switching systems, telephone sets, telex and messageswitching systems, coaxial cables, micro wave systems, optical fibres, satellite communication systems, launch and space vehicles, earth stations, datacom systems. *Operations:* telephone, telex and satellite systems, datacom services.
3. Film	Feature theatrical film Feature TV film Video tapes/discs
4. Publishing	Newspapers Magazines Books Educational materials
5. News	Printnews Photonews Filmnews
6. Record	Records Tapes Cassettes Videodiscs
7. Advertising	Promotional messages/campaigns
8. Consumer Electronics	Radio/TV receiving sets, gramophones, recorders VTR equipment
9. Electronic Components	Transistors Integrated circuits
10. Paper	Newspaper-print Magazine-print Book-print

In addition to these 10 key sectors there are some less voluminous or less distinguishable activities, such as broadcasting, production of office machinery (copiers, typewriters), and manufacturing of assorted support technologies, such as printing machinery, cameras, studio equipment, radio-TV senders, and unprocessed film.

110

Table 3
Foreign Activities of Information Corporations

Rank[1]	Corporation	Foreign Sales %[2]	Number of Countries Where Corporation Holds Foreign Subsidiaries[3]
1	AT&T	22.5 (est)	1
2	IBM	50	45
3	Philips	80 (est)	n/a
4	GT&E	22 (1978)	36
5	Matsushita	31	33
6	RCA	16.5	4
7	Xerox	44	19
8	IT&T	49*	19
9	International Paper	22.1 (1978)	3
10	General Electric	22	6
11	Siemens	50*	25
12	AEG/Telefunken	44	21
13	Hitachi	20	6
14	Reed International	45	1
15	Sperry Rand	44.8	13
16	CBS	14.6	30
17	Rockwell	21*	10
18	Thomson-Brandt	35.6	9
19	NCR	49	10
20	Burroughs	42	22
21	Nippon Electric	24	3
22	Sony	59	n/a
23	Rank Xerox	n/a	20
24	Control Data	34	25
25	Honeywell	32	24
26	ABC	20 (est)	1
27	Ericsson	85	27
28	EMI	65	28
29	Lockheed	26.2*	4
30	Fujitsu	11.4	12
31	Litton	24	5
32	Northern Telecom	n/a	5
33	Olivetti	48.6	30
34	TRW	34*	14
35	Grundig	46	8
36	Plessey	51	9
37	Hachette	14	3
38	CGE	36*	18
39	Bertelsmann	25.9	13
40	Warner Communications	21.2 (est)	9
41	Time Inc.	14	13
42	Digital Equipment	37.5	4
43	Polygram	75 (est)	n/a
44	MCA	19	1
45	Texas Instruments	10 (1977)	11
46	Bosch	51*	21
47	CII-Honeywell Bull	n/a	n/a

Table 3 (continued)

Rank[1]	Corporation	Foreign Sales %[2]	Number of Countries Where Corporation Holds Foreign Subsidiaries[3]
48	Gulf & Western	16*	3
49	McDonnel Douglas	37.7*	n/a
50	ICL	40	18
51	McGraw Hill	20 (est)	6
52	Sanyo	55	n/a
53	LTV	n/a	4
54	New York Times	30 (est)	1
55	Toshiba	17*	n/a
56	Singer	44*	11
57	Rank Organization	60	\5
58	Nixdorf	n/a	n/a
59	Transamerica	32	2
60	Washington Post	20 (est)	n/a
61	20th Century Fox	44.5	2
62	Decca	60.4	n/a
63	Columbia Pictures	30.7	n/a
64	Thomson Organization	14	9
65	News International	15 (est)	2
66	S. Pearson	38	3
67	Nielsen	41	22
68	J.W. Thompson	49	20
69	Disney Productions	40	4
70	COMSAT	n/a	n/a
71	Young & Rubicam	39	n/a
72	McCann Erickson	66.8	47 (Interpublic)
73	MGM	11 (est)	n/a
74	Ogilvy & Mather	50.9	28
75	ATV/ACC	25 (est)	5
76	Playboy	17.6	3
77	Burnett	30	5
78	Associated Press	20	**
79	BBDO	34.3	14
80	SSC&B	76	n/a
81	Bates	52.7	n/a
82	Reuters	80	**
83	UPI (1977)	20	**
84	D'Arcy McManus	46.7	n/a
85	Foote & Cone	31.4	n/a
86	AFP	21	**

[1] Corporations are ranked as in Table 1.

[2] Wherever possible percentages of foreign sales were calculated or estimated for the corporations' information sales. In cases where foreign sales were available only for total sales this is indicated with *
Foreign sales include exports from the home country plus sales of overseas affiliates.

[3] Those subsidiaries were taken that are wholly owned or in which the parent holds over 75% of the stock.

** The news agencies form a somewhat special category since they have their corresponding bureaus in an exceptionally large number of countries.

Table 4
Data Processing Sales (1977)[1]

Rank	Corporation	Sales in $ Millions
1	IBM	14,765
2	Burroughs	1,884
3	NCR	1,574
4	CDC	1,513
5	Sperry Rand	1,472
6	Digital Equipment	1,059
7	Honeywell	1,037
8	Fujitsu	856
9	CII-Honeywell Bull	765
10	Hitachi	720
11	Siemens	550
12	Olivetti	499 (est.)
13	NEC	400
14	Nixdorf	384
15	Philips	376 (est.)
16	TRW	350
17	ICL	233
18	Xerox	209
19	General Electric	200
20	Texas Instruments	160
21	CGE	129 (est.)
22	McDonnell Douglas	112
23	GT&E	75
24	Litton	70
		29,352

[1]Source: Corporations' Annual Reports

Table 5
Mainframe Computer Sales (1979)[1]

Rank	Corporation	Sales in $ Millions
1	IBM	18,338
2	Burroughs	2,432
3	NCR	2,404
4	Control Data	2,273
5	Sperry Rand	2,270
6	Honeywell	1,453

[1]Source: *Datamation*, July 1980

Table 6
Minicomputer Sales (1979)[1]

Rank	Corporation	Sales in $ Millions
1	Digital Equipment	2,031.6
2	Hewlett Packard*	1,030
3	Nixdorf	722
4	Data General*	539.6
5	Texas Instruments	425

[1]Source: *Datamation*, July 1980
*Hewlett Packard and Data General do not appear on the list of "86."

Table 7
Peripheral Equipment Sales (1979)[1]

Rank	Corporation	Sales in $ Millions
1	Memorex*	664
2	Storage Technology*	479.5
3	Xerox	475
4	TRW	440
5	3M*	310
6	Northern Telecom	300
7	IT&T	260

[1]Source: *Datamation*. July 1980
*Memorex, Storage Technology and 3M do not appear on the list of the "86."

Table 8
Software and Services Sales (1977)[1]

Rank	Corporation	Sales in $ Millions
1	Computer Sciences	416.1
2	Automatic Data Processing	400.8
3	General Electric*	350
4	Electronic Data Systems	311.5
5	McDonnell Douglas*	253

[1]Source: *Datamation*, July 1980
*Only General Electric and McDonnell Douglas appear on the list of "86."

Table 9
Telecommunication Sales (1976)[1]
(Telephone Systems)

Rank	a) Equipment Manufacturers	Sales in $ Millions
1	Western Electric (sub. of AT&T)	5,900
2	IT&T	3,200
3	Hitachi	1,830
4	Siemens	1,800
5	Thomson-Brandt	1,413 (est.)
6	GT&E	1,328
7	Ericsson	1,300
8	Northern Telecom	1,128
9	Rockwell	892
10	NEC	800
11	CGE	700
12	Plessey	648
13	Philips	600
14	Matsushita	508
15	Fujitsu	128
16	Olivetti	64 (est.)
		22,239

[1]Source: Corporations' Annual Reports

Table 10
Telecommunication Sales (1976)[1]

Rank	b) Satellite Manufacturers	Sales in $ Millions
1	General Electric	2,099
2	Lockheed	1,210
3	Rockwell	935
4	Sperry Rand	526
5	IT&T	521
6	ITV	502
7	McDonnell Douglas	483
8	Honeywell	428
9	RCA	368
10	Singer	364
11	TRW	330
12	Plessey	109
		7,875

[1]Source: Corporations' Annual Reports

Table 11
Data/Communication Equipment Sales (1979)[1]

Rank	Corporation	Sales in $ Millions
1	IBM	157.7
2	Racal-Milgo*	121
3	NCR	81.5
4	Motorola*	81.3
5	Memorex*	58.9
6	3M*	48.9
7	Control Data	40
8	Northern Telecom	30
9	Hewlett-Packard*	29.5
10	Burroughs	28.3
11	Sperry Rand	23.7
12	Honeywell	14.5
13	Rockwell	5.0

[1]Source: *Datamation*, July 1980

*Racal-Milgo, Motorola, Memorex, 3M, and Hewlett Packard are not on the "86" lists.

Table 12
Data Communication Carriers Revenues (1979)[1]

Rank	Corporation	Revenue in $ Millions
1	AT&T	2,309
2	GT&E	797.6
3	Western Union Corporation*	451.2
4	IT&T	169.7
5	United Telecommunications*	68
6	COMSAT	16.2
7	RCA	15.8

[1] Source: *Datamation*, August 1980

* Western Union Corporation and United Telecommunications do not appear on the list of "86."

Table 13
Production and Distribution Sales of Feature Films for TV (1976)[1]

Rank	Corporation	Sales in $ Thousands
1	MCA	249,658
2	Columbia Pictures	104,600
3	EMI	80,432
4	Gulf & Western	65,000
5	Warner Communications	63,540
6	ATV/ACC	62,932
7	MGM	57,400
8	Transamerica	56,657
9	Time Inc.	54,700
10	20th Century Fox	37,687
11	Disney Productions	18,808
		851,414

[1] Source: Corporations' Annual Reports

116

Table 14
Production of Theatrical Films Sales (1976)[1]

Rank	Corporation	Sales in $ Thousands
1	20th Century Fox	254,910
2	Transamerica	230,404
3	Warner Communications	221,649
4	MCA	213,433
5	EMI	160,299
6	Columbia Pictures	153,500
7	Gulf & Western	152,000
8	Rank Organization	112,504
9	Disney Productions	100,325
10	MGM	47,600
11	ATV/ACC	25,446
12	ABC	5,084
		1,677,154

[1] Source: Corporations' Annual Reports

Table 15
Record Sales (1976)[1]

Rank	Corporation	Sales in $ Thousands
1	EMI	743,205
2	Polygram	714,286
3	Matsushita	691,066
4	CBS	563,800
5	RCA	500,000
6	Warner Communications	406,062
7	ABC	187,584
8	Decca	162,646 (est.)
9	MCA	112,378
10	Transamerica	86,873
11	Bertelsmann	67,402 (est.)
12	Columbia Pictures	42,100
13	ATV/ACC	19,978
14	Disney Productions	12,173
15	20th Century Fox	9,936
16	Playboy	2,000
		4,321,489

[1] Source: Corporations' Annual Reports

Table 16
Advertising Agencies Income (1976)[1]

Rank	Agency	Revenue in $ Thousands
1	J.W. Thompson	155.8
2	Young & Rubicam	139.8
3	McCann Erickson	133.6
4	Burnett	106.3
5	Ogilvy & Mather	106
6	BBDO	96.4
7	SSC&B	96
8	Bates	93.5
9	D'Arcy McManus	72
10	Foote & Cone	68.2
		1,027.6

[1] Source: *Advertising Age* 1976 Survey

Table 17
Publishing Sales (1976)[1]

Rank	Corporation	Sales in $ Thousands
1	Reed International (n + m + b)	619,402
2	Time Inc. (m + b)	556,000
3	S. Pearson (b + n)	523,565
4	McGraw Hill (b + e + m)	426,614
5	New York Times (n + m)	404,343
6	Hachette (n + m + b)	391,395
7	Bertelsmann (m + b)	342,063
8	W. Post (n + m + b)	322,791
9	RCA (b)	314,000 (est.)
10	Thomson Organization (n + b)	297,955
11	Xerox (e)	250,000
12	IT&T (e + b)	235,282
13	CBS (b + m)	220,800
14	News International (n)	201,034
15	Playboy (m)	106,254
16	Gulf & Western (b)	71,000
17	Litton (e)	57,888
18	Singer (e)	55,300
19	Warner Communications (b)	48,407
20	ABC (b)	31,178
21	Disney Productions (m + e)	28,833
22	MCA (b)	9,000 (est.)
		5,513,104

[1] Source: Corporations' Annual Reports.

n = newspaper

m = magazine

b = book

e = educational material

Table 18
Consumer Electronics Sales (1976)[1]

Rank	Corporation	Sales in $ Thousands
1	Matsushita	3,947,802
2	Philips	3,587,970
3	Hitachi	2,366,000
4	Sony	1,505,122
5	Grundig	945,980
6	AEG/Telefunken	936,493
7	RCA	871,000
8	GT&E	728,688
9	General Electric	706,378 (est.)
10	IT&T	705,846 (est.)
11	Sanyo	530,528
12	Rockwell	504,000
13	Shibaura	445,993
14	Bosch	400,000 (est.)
15	Thomson-Brandt	318,020 (est.)
16	Rank Organization	302,728
17	Nippon Electric	162,665
18	Decca	162,646 (est.)
19	EMI	116,581 (est.)
20	Plessey	45,824
		19,290,264

[1] Source: Corporations' Annual Reports

Table 19
Electronic Components: Integrated Circuits Sales (1975)[1]

Rank	Corporation	Sales in $ Millions
1	Texas Instruments	290
2	Fairchild*	160
3	National Semiconductor*	150
4	Philips	150
5	Motorola*	120
6	Intel*	110
7	Toshiba	100
8	Nippon Electric	100
9	RCA	90
10	Siemens	40
11	Plessey	10

[1] Source: S. Nora and A. Minc. "L'informatisation de la société," Annexe, Industrie et services informatiques. p. 77; J. M. Quatrepoint, "Composants électroniques," Le Monde, April 19, 1977.

* Fairchild, National Semiconductor, Motorola and Intel are not on the list of "86."

Table 20
Paper Industry Sales (1976)[1]

Rank	Corporation	Sales in $ Millions
1	International Paper (U.S.)	3,450
2	Reed International (U.K.)	1,832 (est.)
3	McMillan Bloedel (Canada)	1,542
4	Scott Paper (U.S.)	1,373
5	Svenska Tändsticks (Sweden)	1,061
6	Moore (Canada)	1,053
7	Svenska Cellulosa (Sweden)	953
8	Papierwerke Waldhof Aschaffenburg (F.R.G.)	609

[1] Source: *Fortune's* listing of largest industrial corporations in 1976

Table 21a
Photocopying Equipment Sales (1976)[1]

Rank	Corporation	Sales in $ Millions
1	Xerox	3,600
2	IBM	1,000
3	Olivetti	47.7
4	Litton	0.2

[1] Source: Corporations' Annual Reports

Table 21b
Broadcasting Equipment Sales (1976)[1]

Rank	Corporation	Sales in $ Millions
1	AEG/Telefunken	454.8
2	Philips	345.6 (est.)
3	RCA	250 (est.)
4	EMI	116.5 (est.)

[1] Source: Corporations' Annual Reports

Table 22
World Market for Records (1977)[1]

Rank	Corporation	Sales in $ Millions
1	CBS	786
2	EMI	753
3	Polygram	750
4	Warner Communications	532
5	RCA	400
6	MCA	100
7	United Artists	93
8	Bertelsmann	92
9	ABC	72

[1] Source: *Billboard Buyer's Guide,* September 1978

Table 23
Semiconductors Sales (1975)[1]

Rank	Corporation	Sales in $ Millions
1	Texas Instruments	550
2	Philips	400
3	Motorola*	350
4	Fairchild*	250
5	Toshiba	220
6	National Semiconductor*	200
7	Nippon Electric	200
8	RCA	160
9	Siemens	120

[1] Source: J. M. Quatrepoint, "Composant électroniques: peut-on encore sauver l'industrie francaise?," in *Le Monde,* April 19, 1977.

* Motorola, Fairchild, and National Semiconductor do not appear on the list of "86."

Table 24
Concentration Ratio in Sectors (1976)[1]

Sector	%
Dataprocessing	71
Telecommunications (telephony systems)	56
Telecommunications (satellites)	57
TV-film	52
Theatrical film	43
Records	51
Publishing	40
Advertising	42
Consumer Electronics	52
Electronic Components	51
Paper	52

[1] Sales of the three largest corporations as % of the ten largest in the world.

Table 25
Information Corporations Among the 50 Leading U.S. Exporters (1979)[1]

Rank	Corporation	Exports in $ Thousands	% of Total Sales
1	General Electric	2,772,100	12.34
2	McDonnell Douglas	1,788,425	33.88
3	Lockheed	956,000	23.49
4	Raytheon*	734,000	19.69
5	Rockwell	536,000	8.29
6	International Paper	283,000	6.15
7	Warner Communications	253,368	15.37
8	TRW	251,700	5.52
9	Harris*	247,900	25.24
10	Motorola*	211,531	7.79

[1] Source: *Fortune,* September 22, 1980.

* Raytheon, Harris, and Motorola are not on the "86" list.

121

Table 26
Information Corporations Advertising Expenditures in 1979[1]

Rank	Corporation	Advertising in $ Millions
1	AT&T	219.8
2	Gulf & Western	191.5
3	RCA	158.6
4	CBS	146.1
5	General Electric	139.4
6	IT&T	132.4
7	Time Inc.	102.4
8	Transamerica	95
9	MCA	66
10	Warner Communications	57.6
11	ABC	42
12	IBM	31.1

[1] Source: *Advertising Age*, September 11, 1980.

Table 27
Sample of Executive Salaries in the Information Industry (U.S. Corporations, 1979)[1]

Name	Position	Salary
The New York Times Company		
Arthur Sulzberger	Chairman	$ 393,855
Sydney Gruson	Vice Chairman	$ 276,866
Walter Mattson	President	$ 271,364
James Goodale	Vice Chairman	$ 252,409
John Pomfret	Senior Vice President	$ 188,894
Playboy Enterprises Inc.		
Hugh Hefner	Chairman	$ 301,000
Derick Daniels	President	$ 476,000
Marvin Huston	Senior Vice President	$ 231,819
Victor Lownes	President, Playboy Clubs	$ 614,608
Nat Lehrman	Senior Vice President	$ 189,000
Time Inc.		
Andrew Heiskell	Chairman	$ 507,550
James Shepley	President	$ 450,150
Arthur Temple	Vice Chairman	$ 396,550
J. Richard Munro	Executive Vice President	$ 282,131
Charles Bear	Group Vice President	$ 324,050
CBS Inc.		
William Paley	Chairman	$ 789,109
John Backe	President	$ 732,312
Gene Jankowski	Vice President	$ 363,309
John Purcell	Executive Vice President	$ 345,812
Walter Yetnikoff	Vice President	$ 215,000

Table 27 (continued)

Name	Position	Salary
RCA Inc.		
Edgar Griffiths	President, Chief Executive Officer	$ 428,750
Jane Pfeiffer	Chairman	$ 291,667
Roy Pollack	Executive Vice President	$ 238,750
Julius Koppelman	Executive Vice President	$ 235,833
George Fuchs	Executive Vice President	$ 210,000
Columbia Pictures Industries Inc.		
Leo Jaffe	Chairman	$ 221,000
Francis Vincent, Jr.	President	$ 247,000
Robert Stone	Chief Operating Officer	$ 187,596
Joseph Fischer	Executive Vice President	$ 188,750
Twentieth Century-Fox Film Corporation		
Dennis Stanfill	Chairman	$ 655,098
Alan Ladd, Jr.	Senior Vice President	$ 269,238
Alan Livingston	Senior Vice President	$ 342,437
Edwin Bowen	Senior Vice President	$ 199,585
Walt Disney Productions		
Ronald Miller	Executive Vice President	$ 136,152
Richard Nunis	Vice President	$ 110,166
Donn Tatum	Chairman	$ 244,868
E. Cardon Walker	President	$ 244,868
Warner Communications Inc.		
Steven Ross	Chairman	+ $3,865,809
Jay Emmet	Office of the President	$ 469,330
Emanuel Gerard	Office of the President	$ 469,330
David Horowitz	Office of the President	$ 469,330
Bert Wasserman	Senior Vice President	$ 418,616

+ Annual salary is $350,000. In 1979 there was a bonus of $3,515,809

[1] Source: *Communication Perspectives*, vol. 3, No. 4, August 1980.

Table 28
A Selection of Highest Budgeted Films in 1977–1980[1]

Close Encounters of the Third Kind (Columbia 1977)	$20,000,000
A Bridge Too Far (Joseph Levine, 1977)	$24,000,000
Superman (Warner Bros. 1978)	$25,000,000
Moonraker (United Artists, 1979)	$32,000,000
Star Trek (Paramount, 1979)	$40,000,000 (Approx.)
Heaven's Gate (United Artists, 1980)	$40,000,000 (Approx.)

[1] Source: *Variety*, August 29, 1979

Table 29
R&D Expenditures in % of Total Sales for Data Processing Corporations (1976)[1]

Rank	Corporation	R&D Expenditures $ Millions	% of Sales
1	IBM	1,012	6.2
2	Sperry Rand	158.9	5
3	Honeywell	125.6	5
4	Burroughs	107.6	5.8
5	NCR	94.3	4.1
6	Control Data	58.9	4.4
7	Digital Equipment	58.4	7.9

[1] Source: *Business Week*, June 27, 1977

Table 30
Ratios of Long-Term Debt/Assets

Corporation	%	Borrowing Record
AT&T	37	H
IBM	2	VL
General Electric	11	M
Philips	14	M
Matsushita	3.1	VL
IT&T	21	M-H
GT&E	39	H
RCA	17	M
Xerox	22	M-H
Siemens	17	M
AEG/Telefunken	22	M-H
Hitachi	17.3	M
Sperry Rand	20	M-H
CBS	7	L
Rockwell	19	M
NCR	27	M-H
Burroughs	8.6	L
Nippon Electric	27	M-H
EMI	30	M-H
Control Data	35	H
Honeywell	10	L
ABC	22	M-H
Ericsson	22	M-H
Fujitsu	10	L
Litton	10	L
Northern Telecom	37	H
Olivetti	27	M-H
TRW	20	M-H
Hachette	6	L
Plessey	13	M
Grundig	18	M
CGE	19	M

Table 30 (continued)

Corporation	%	Borrowing Record
Bertelsmann	8.4	L
Warner Communications	29	M-H
Time Inc.	15	M
Digital Equipment	11	M
Texas Instruments	3.3	VL
Gulf & Western	29	M-H
McDonnell Douglas	6	L
McGraw Hill	8.5	L
LTV	54	H
New York Times	2.5	VL
Singer	28	M-H
Rank Organization	20	M-H
Transamerica	13	M
Washington Post	11	M
20th Century Fox	28	M-H
Columbia Pictures	26	M-H
S. Pearson	13	M
J.W. Thompson	3	VL
COMSAT	23	M-H
MGM	40	H
Playboy	10	L
Lockheed	27	M-H

VL=very light borrower
 L=light borrower
 M=moderate borrower
M-H=moderate to heavy borrower
 H=heavy borrower

Table 31
Information Corporations and Their Finance Companies

Corporation	Finance Company	Revenue
Transamerica	Transamerica Finance Co. Bankers Mortgage Co. of Calif. Comp. Européenne de Banque (in 1979 Transamerica is the 10th largest diversified financial company in the U.S. with a net income of $240 million)	
Control Data	various commercial credit services	$423 million
RCA	CIT Financial Corp.	$147 million (1979)
General Electric	General Electric Credit Co.	in 1979: net income $59 million

Table 31 (continued)

Corporation	Finance Company	Revenue
MCA	Columbia Savings and Loans Association	$56 million
IT&T	IT&T Financial Corp.	$46 million (1976)
McDonnell Douglas	McDonnell Douglas Finance	$11 million (1976)
Honeywell	Honeywell Finance Inc.	$9 million (1976)
Time Inc.	Sabine Investment Co. Lumbermen's Investment Co.	$3.8 million (1976)
Gulf & Western	Associates First Capital Corp.	
Rockwell	Rockwell International Credit Corp. Admiral Credit Corp.	
Litton	Litton Industries Credit Corp.	
Warner Communications	Garden State National Bank (63% of the stock)	
Thomson-Brandt	Société Financière Electrique de Banque	
S. Pearson	Lazard Brothers & Co.	
Plessey	Plessey International Finance Corp.	
Siemens	Siemens Finanzierungsgesellschaft für Informationstechnik	
Grundig	Grundig Bank	

Table 32
Finance Companies Owned by Information Corporations on the List of the U.S. Top Ten Finance Companies[1]

Ranking Top Ten	Corporation	Total Financing $ Millions	Net Income $ Millions
1	CIT Financial	4,467	53
2	Control Data	4,402	32
4	Gulf & Western Associates Corp.	2,641	25
8	IT&T Financial	2,182	34
9	Transamerica Financial	760	17

[1] Source: Corporate Data Exchange, *Handbook Banking & Finance*, New York 1980.

Table 33
Transnational Computer-Communication Systems

Applications	Type System	Type Traffic	Type Data	Example	Reasons	Users
coordination corporate management	centralized processing/computer to central computer	bulk transfer	production/marketing accounting/funds personnel/payroll	IBM	large volume-transport &	transnational firms
banking and credit control	distributed networks/computer to computer & men to computer	interactive + data transmission	customer transfer banks transfer foreign exchange bond, stock and share/credit letters	S.W.I.F.T.	resource sharing/ volume + speed/ validation + security	banks/credit bureaux
reservations	distributed networks/computer to computer & men to computer	interactive + data transmission	personal records availability reserv.	SITA	resource sharing	airlines-travel agencies
databanks	remote access (tele-processing) time-sharing men to computer	interactive + data processing	scientific/tech. data simulation models economic data general data	CERN General Electric Lockheed	resource sharing/ volume of data processing/ access to information	scientists government business community
international govern. cooperation	distributed networks/men to computer	interactive + data transmission	meteorol, data criminal records	World Meteor. Org. INTERPOL	resource sharing/ information exchange	government inter-govern. organization
public tele-communication	message switching/men-to-computer-to-men	message transmission	telephone/telex messages	RCA Globcom	large volume transport/speed/ reliable performance	general

Table 34
Shares of Foreign Earnings in U.S. Banks 1970 and 1977

Rank	Corporation	1970 (% of Total Earning)	1977 (% of Total Earning)
1	Citicorp.	40	82.2
2	J.P. Morgan	25	54.5
3	Chase Manhattan	22	64.9
4	Bankamerica	15	34.2
5	Bankers Trust	14.5	79
6	Manufacturers Hanover	13	72
7	Charter New York	12	56.5
8	Chemical New York	10	44.2
9	Wells Fargo	9	27.8
10	First National Boston	8	38.7

Sources: For 1970 data, "International Debt, the Banks and the U.S. Foreign Policy," a report for the Subcommittee on Foreign Economic Policy of the U.S. Senate Committee on Foreign Relations, Washington, 1977.

For 1977 data, *Banking & Finance, CDE Handbook,* New York, 1980.

Table 35
Interlocks Between Diversified-Financial Company of *American Express* and Information Corporations (1977)

Corporation	American Express Direct	Indirect
ABC		2
AT&T	1	17
CBS		4
General Electric	1	9
GT&E		1
IBM	1	21
IT&T		4
RCA		1
Transamerica		1
Honeywell		3
LTV		1
McGraw Hill	1	2
New York Times		6
Rockwell		2
Singer		1
Sperry Rand		4
J.W. Thompson		1
TIme Inc.	1	4
Warner Communications	1	
Lockheed		8
Xerox	2	
COMSAT		1

Table 36
Voting Stock by Institutional Investors in U.S. Information Corporations (1979)

Corporation	Institutional Investors		Commercial Banks	
	No.	% Stock	No.	% Stock
ABC	60	44.42	22	12.50
AT&T	22	5.86	15	3.68
Burroughs	68	50.51	19	19.10
CBS	63	34.16	25	9.36
Disney Productions	40	33.21	15	19.58
General Electric	46	19.25	23	11.58
GT&E	43	16.71	10	4.21
Honeywell	42	26.71	20	9.55
IBM	59	25.16	35	17.94
IT&T	44	19.61	20	10.13
LTV	12	20.94	2	8.11
MCA	27	20.13	9	3.20
McDonnell Douglas	21	38.50	7	4.17
McGraw Hill	35	30.71	15	8.77
NCR	34	36.24	12	10.39
New York Times	9	29.98	3	2.69
Nielsen	20	13.81	12	7.84
RCA	40	15.38	18	3.68
Rockwell	17	24.48	6	19.80
Singer	11	6.95	3	0.81
Sperry Rand	46	34.95	20	14.36
Time Inc.	26	24.36	8	6.41
Transamerica	19	9.25	6	2.38
TRW	39	35.13	16	20.53
Washington Post	13	41.68	1	12.26
Xerox	57	32.78	23	17.51

Source: See note 44, p. 91.

Table 37
Percentage of Voting Stock in Ten Largest Institutional Investors in Japanese Information Corporations (1977)

Corporation	% Voting Stock 10 Largest Institutional Investors	Banks	
		No.	% Voting Stock
Toshiba	31.30	4	6.9
Matsushita	31.10	4	11.4
Hitachi	22.5	4	8.3
Sanyo	32.1	2	7.4
Nippon Electric	44.1	4	17.6
Fujitsu	58.9	3	14.6

Source: Dodwell Marketing Consultants, 1978

Table 38
Family and Individual Interests in Information Corporations

Corporation	Family/Individual	% Voting Stock
Bosch	Bosch	10.5
Bertelsmann	G. Bucerius	10.74
Grundig	Grundig	10.6
Thomson Organization	Thomson	81.3
S. Pearson	Pearson	controlling interest
News International	Murdoch	id.
ATV/ACC	L. Grade	27.5
Decca	E. Lewis	9.54
Control Data	Norris	2.37
Columbia Pictures	K. Kerkorian	6.21
	Allen	5.22
	Rosenham	9.01
McGraw Hill	McGraw	18.73
New York Times	Sulzberger	39.51
Nielsen	Nielsen	58.43
Rockwell	Rockwell	3.51
Time Inc.	Luce	10.95
Washington Post	Graham	23.99
	W. E. Buffett	11.74
Disney Productions	Disney	7.40
MCA	Stein	29.06
CBS	Paley	6.31
Interpublic	W. E. Buffett	19.29
J.W. Thompson	W. E. Buffett	2.48
McDonnell Douglas	McDonnell	17.49
MGM	K. Kerkorian	47.00

Table 39
Interlocking Directorates of the Six New York Banks (Chase Manhattan Bank, Chemical New York, Citibank, Morgan Guaranty Trust, Manufacturers Hanover Trust and Bankers Trust) and U.S. Information Corporations

Corporation	No. of Direct Interlocks	No. of Indirect Interlocks
ABC	2	21
AT&T	5	101
CBS	2	41
General Electric	7	42
IBM	8	66
RCA	1	31
New York Times	2	15
Lockheed	9	21
Sperry Rand	3	21
Time Inc.	2	20
Xerox	2	24

Source: See note 44, p. 91.

Table 40

Interlocking Directorates Between Information Corporations and Banks in Japan

Corporation	Bank	No. of Directors
Fujitsu	Dai Ichi Kangyo Bank	3
Hitachi	Dai Ichi Kangyo Bank	2
Matsushita	Sumitomo Bank	1
	Industrial Bank of Japan	1
Nippon Electric	Sumitomo Bank	3
Sanyo	Sumitomo Bank	3
	Kyowa Bank	1
Toshiba	Mitsui Bank	1

Source: Dodwell Marketing Consultants, 1978.

Table 41

Voting Stock of U.S. Commercial Banks in U.S. Information Corporations (1977)

Corporation	% Voting Stock 25 Top Shareholders	Banks Among 25 Top Shareholders No.	Banks Among 25 Top Shareholders % Voting Stock	4 Banks with Largest % Voting Stock	
ABC	35.07	5	8.31	Morgan	2.65
				First Dallas	1.91
				Bankers Trust	1.90
				Provident N.	.97
AT&T	5.86	15	3.68	Bankers Trust	.49
				Manuf. Hanover	.37
				Mellon	.35
				First Boston	.29
Burroughs	36.28	9	10.39	Morgan	3.09
				Harris	2.61
				Manuf. Hanover	.62
				Citicorp.	.72
CBS	32.55	6	5.79	Chemical	1.50
				Fidelity Bank	1.06
				Bank of America	.93
				Bankers Trust	.89
Disney Productions	36.79	10	18.81	Morgan	4.77
				Bankers Trust	2.50
				Bank of America	1.89
				Mellon	1.78
General Electric	14.98	14	9.94	Morgan	1.30
				Citibank	1.24
				First Boston	1.16
				Bankers Trust	1.10
GT&E	14.10	7	4.01	N. Detroit	1.31
				Citibank	.74
				Harris	.74
				Bank of America	.44

Table 41 (continued)

Corporation	% Voting Stock 25 Top Shareholders	Banks Among 25 Top Shareholders		4 Banks with Largest % Voting Stock	
		No.	% Voting Stock		
Honeywell	22.64	8	7.55	Citibank	2.20
				Bankers Trust	1.20
				F.N. Boston	1.01
				Hartford	.97
IBM	18.14	17	14.22	Morgan	2.53
				Citibank	1.44
				Manuf. Hanover	1.23
				Bankers Trust	1.20
IT&T	16.49	8	8.39	Morgan	2.13
				Chase Manhattan	1.49
				Harris	1.47
				Nat. Detroit	1.37
LTV	20.73	1	8.11	First City Bank of Dallas	8.11
MCA	49.17	7	3.20	Chemical	2.30
				Pittsburgh N.B.	.58
				U.S. Trust	.15
				Bank of America	.15
McDonnell Douglas	56.13	7	4.71	Bankers Trust	—
				Morgan	1.47
				Chase Manhattan	1.13
				First Union Bank	.41
McGraw Hill	46.94	7	7.19	Savings Bank Trust	2.27
				Bankers Trust	1.41
				Boatmens N.B.	1.04
				F.N.B. Boston	.75
NCR	34.58	9	10.19	Winter N.B.	1.81
				Chase Manhattan	1.76
				Wachovia Bank	1.76
				Morgan	1.50
New York Times	69.49	3	2.69	Lehman Bros.	2.19
				Chase Manhattan	.40
Nielsen	72.24	12	7.84	Nat. Boulevard	1.88
				Harris	1.64
				Morgan	1.27
				Bank of America	.85

Table 41 (continued)

Corporation	% Voting Stock 25 Top Shareholders	Banks Among 25 Top Shareholders		4 Banks with Largest % Voting Stock	
		No.	% Voting Stock		
RCA	13.63	7	2.68	Bank of America	.80
				Savings Bank Trust	.55
				Hartford	.31
				Bankers Trust	.30
Rockwell	28.84	6	19.80	Western Banc.	17.32
				Rep. Nat. Bank of Dallas	1.54
				Mellon	.60
				Continental Illinois	.27
Singer	6.95	3	.81	Lehman Bros.	.30
				Bank of America	.29
				Wachovia Bank	.22
Sperry Rand	30.26	8	12.12	Morgan	3.82
				Chase Manhattan	2.55
				Continental Illinois	1.78
				Chemical	1.10
Time Inc.	42.76	8	6.41	Morgan	2.96
				Chase Manhattan	.82
				First City N.B.	.80
				Bank of America	.52
Transamerica	10.45	6	2.38	Bank of America	.81
				North Carolina	.39
				Boatmens N.B.	.36
				F.W. Nat. Bank	.29
TRW	31.35	12	9.42	Nat. City Corp.	1.45
				First Chicago	1.13
				Cleve Trust	1.00
				Northern Trust	.84
Washington Post	78.41	1	12.26	Morgan	12.26
Xerox	25.65	10	15.01	Citibank	4.09
				F.N.B.	2.67
				Morgan	1.41
				N.B. Detroit	1.29

Source: See note 44, p. 91.

Table 42
Lead Banks Domestic Borrowing United States Information Corporations

Corporation	Bank
ABC	Manufacturers Hanover Bankers Trust Chemical Bank
Control Data	Chase Manhattan Security Pacific Chemical Bank Continental Illinois Citibank Bank of America
Digital Equipment	Morgan Guaranty Trust
20th Century Fox	F.N.B. Boston Security Pacific Manufacturers Hanover Wells Fargo
General Electric	Citibank Morgan Guaranty Trust
Honeywell	Bank of America Security Pacific
IT&T	Chase Manhattan Philadelphia N.B. Eur-Am Bank Continental Illinois
Litton	Wells Fargo Morgan Guaranty Trust Continental Illinois Bank of America Bankers Trust Chase Manhattan Chemical Bank
Lockheed	Bankers Trust Bank of America
MCA	Bank of America F.N.B. Chicago Crocker N.B.
New York Times	Morgan Guaranty Trust
RCA	Chase Manhattan Manufacturers Hanover Morgan Guaranty Trust

Table 42 (continued)

Corporation	Bank
Rockwell	Morgan Guaranty Trust
	Citibank
	Mellon Bank
	Bank of America
	Chase Manhattan
	Chemical Bank
	F.N.B. Chicago
Singer	Morgan Guaranty Trust
	Bank of America
	Chemical Bank
	Chase Manhattan
	Citibank
	Manufacturers Hanover
Sperry Rand	Citibank
	Manufacturers Hanover
	Eur-Am Bank
	Continental Illinois
	N.B. of Detroit
Warner Communications	F.N.B. Boston
	Chase Manhattan
	Continental Illinois
	Manufacturers Hanover
	Security Pacific
Western Electric (Subs. AT&T)	Chemical Bank

Source: R. B. Cohen, op. cit., 1979

Table 43
Lead Banks International Borrowing United States Information Corporations

Corporation	Bank
Control Data	Mellon Bank Eur-Am Bank
20th Century Fox	Lehman Bros. Paribas
General Electric	Morgan Guaranty Trust Stanley Goldman Sachs Union de Banque Suisse Société de Banque Suisse
Honeywell	Société de Banque Suisse Union de Banque Suisse Swiss Credit Bank
IBM	Mitsubishi Bank Bank of Tokyo Dai Ichi Kangyo Bank Fuji Bank Mitsui Bank Sumitomo Bank
IT&T	Banque Nationale de Paris Lazard Frères Co.
Litton	Union de Banque Suisse Western-Am. Bank Continental Illinois
MCA	Dresdner Bank Bank of America
NCR	Swiss Credit Bank Union de Banque Suisse Bank of Nova Scotia Deutsche Bank
Rockwell	Morgan Guaranty Trust Mellon Bank
Sperry Rand	Eur-Am Bank Bank of Nova Scotia
Xerox	First Boston Corp Citicorp.

Source: R. B. Cohen, op. cit., 1979.

Table 44
Lead Banks Domestic Borrowing Japanese Information Corporations

Corporation	Bank
Fujitsu	Dai Ichi Kangyo Bank
	Mitsubishi Bank
	Sanwa Bank
Hitachi	Dai Ichi Kangyo Bank
	Sanwa Bank
	Fuji Bank
	Sumitomo Bank
	Citibank
	Bankers Trust
	Union de Banque Suisse
Matsushita	Sumitomo Bank
Nippon Electric	Sumitomo Bank
	Dai Ichi Kangyo Bank
	Citibank
	Chase Manhattan
	Bank of America
	Morgan Guaranty Trust
	Société de Banque Suisse
	Deutsche Bank
Sanyo	Sumitomo Bank
Sony	Mitsui Bank
Toshiba	Mitsui Bank
	Dai Ichi Kangyo Bank
	Fuji Bank
	Sumitomo Bank
	Deutsche Bank
	Chase Manhattan
	Barclays
	Citibank
	National Westminster

Source: R. B. Cohen, op. cit., 1979 and Dodwell Marketing Consultants, 1978.

Table 45
Lead Banks International Borrowing Japanese Information Corporations

Corporation	Bank
Fujitsu	Bank of America Chase Manhattan Lloyds
Hitachi	Citibank Société Generale Bankers Trust
Nippon Electric	Citibank Chase Manhattan Bank of America
Sanyo	Bank of America
Toshiba	Deutsche Bank Chase Manhattan Barclays

Source: R. B. Cohen, op. cit., 1979.

Table 46
Lead Banks International Borrowing West-European Information Corporations

Corporation	Bank
EMI	Lazard Frerès Co.
Reed International	Swiss Credit Corp. Dresdner Bank Deutsche Bank
Bosch	Union de Banque Suisse
Ericsson	Svenska Handelsbanken Société de Banque Suisse Stockholms Enskilda Union de Banque Suisse Deutsche Bank
Olivetti	Commerzbank Eur-Am Bank
Philips	Amro ABN Dresdner Bank Société de Banque Suisse Union de Banque Suisse
CGE	Morgan Guaranty Trust
Siemens	Deutsche Bank Union de Banque Suisse Société de Banque Suisse

Source: See note 44, p. 91.

Table 47
Information Corporations and Type of Control

Corporation	Rationale Classification

1. Category: Significant Owner Control

Bertelsmann (F.R.G.)	G. Bucerius owns 10.74% of the stock
Bosch (F.R.G.)	Fam. Bosch owns 10.5% of the stock
Grundig	Fam. Grundig owns 10.6% of the stock
MCA (U.S.)	Fam. Stein owns 29.06% of the stock
McGraw Hill (U.S.)	Fam. McGraw owns 18.73% of the stock
MGM (U.S.)	K. Kerkorian owns 47% of the stock
New York Times (U.S.)	Fam. Sulzberger owns 39.51% of the stock
Nielsen (U.S.)	Fam. Nielsen owns 58.43% of the stock
Time Inc. (U.S.)	Fam. Luce owns 10.95% of the stock
Interpublic (U.S.)	W. E. Buffett owns 19.29% of the stock
ATV/ACC (U.K.)	L. Grade owns 27.5% of the stock
Decca (U.K.)	E. Lewis owns 9.54% of the stock
News International (U.K.)	R. Murdoch has controlling interest
S. Pearson (U.K.)	Fam. Pearson has controlling interest
Thomson Organization (U.K.)	Fam. Thomson owns 81.3% of the stock

2. Category: Significant Owner Control + Significant Financial Control

Nixdorf (F.R.G.)	H. Nixdorf owns 75% of the stock Deutsche Bank owns 25% of the stock
Columbia Pictures (U.S.)	K. Kerkorian owns 25% of the stock H. Allen (investment bank) owns 25% of the stock
Disney Productions (U.S.)	Fam. Disney owns 7.4% of the stock Banks total 18.83% of the stock The New York Banks own 8.22% of the stock The Mellon Group owns 3.54% of the stock The Bank of America owns 1.84% of the stock and has a director on the board
McDonnell Douglas (U.S.)	Fam. interests own 17.49% of the stock Bankers Trust owns 22.32% of the stock
Washington Post (U.S.)	Fam. Graham owns 23.99% of the stock Morgan owns 12.26% of the stock

3. Category: Significant Financial Control

Hachette (F.R.)	Banks own 14.49% of the stock Paribas owns 4.25% and has one director Union de Banque Suisse owns 5% of the stock
CGE (F.R.)	Groupe de la Caisse Dépots owns 5.76% of the stock
Thomson-Brandt (F.R.)	Banks own 29.8% of the stock Paribas owns 8.31% of the stock Crédit Lyonnais owns 6.01% of the stock

Table 47 (continued)

Corporation	Rationale Classification
Fujitsu (J.)	Banks own 16.2% of the stock Lead supplier Dai Ichi Kangyo Bank owns 9.5% of the stock and has three directors
Matsushita (J.)	Banks own 9.5% of the stock The lead domestic debtholder Sumitomo Bank is the largest stockholder with 5.5% and has one director
Nippon Electric (J.)	Banks own 17.6% of the stock Lead supplier the Sumitomo Group owns 12.5% and has 3 directors
Sanyo (J.)	Banks own 7.4% of the stock The lead supplier Sumitomo owns 4.7% and has three directors The Kyowa Bank owns 2.7% of the stock and has one director
Toshiba (J.)	Banks own 6.9% of the stock The Mitsui Bank is the lead supplier with 17.2% of total borrowings, owns 3.9% of the stock and has one director
ABC (U.S.)	Banks own 8.3% of the stock New York banks own 5.43% of the stock Citibank has one director Moderate to heavy borrowing The lead supplier Manufacturers Hanover Trust has one director
AT&T (U.S.)	The stock is widely dispersed and the New York banks own 1.51% They have seven directors Lead supplier Chemical has two directors Heavy borrowing
Burroughs (U.S.)	Banks own 10% of the stock Morgan is the largest stockholder with 3.09% The New York banks own 4.8% of the stock
General Electric (U.S.)	Moderate borrower Lead suppliers Morgan and Citibank are the two largest stockholders Banks own 9.9% of the widely dispersed stock New York banks own 4.76% of the stock Morgan has three directors Citibank, Chase Manhattan, Manufacturers Hanover Trust and Chemical all have one director There are 11 indirect interlocks with Bankers Trust

Table 47 (continued)

Corporation	Rationale Classification
IBM (U.S.)	Banks own 14.22% of the stock The New York banks own 8.12% of the stock Citibank has three directors Chemical has two directors Bankers Trust has one director and Chase Manhattan has one director The largest stockholder is Morgan with 2.5% of the stock and has one director
LTV (U.S.)	Largest shareholder is the First City Bank of Dallas with 8.11% of the stock; no other stockholder has over 5%
Rockwell (U.S.)	Largest shareholder is Western Bancorporation with 17.32% of the stock and has one director Banks own 19.8% of the stock An important supplier the Mellon Bank has one director
Sperry Rand (U.S.)	Moderate to heavy borrowing Lead supplier Citibank has one director Lead supplier Manufacturers Hanover Trust has two directors Banks own 12.2% of the stock The New York banks own 7.86% of the stock
Xerox (U.S.)	Moderate to heavy borrowing Lead supplier First Boston has 2.67% of the stock Banks own 15.01% of the stock The New York banks own 7.28% of the stock Citibank and Bankers Trust each have one director

4. Category: Moderate Financial Control

Corporation	Rationale Classification
Siemens (F.R.G.)	Lead supplier Deutsche Bank has two directors
Hitachi (J.)	Banks own 8.3% of the stock The Sanwa Bank owns 2.2% of the stock and holds 12.2% of the debt The Dai Ichi Kangyo Bank owns 1.9% of the stock and holds 12.2% of the debt The Industrial Bank of Japan owns 2.3% of the stock and holds 12.7% of the debt

Table 47 (continued)

Corporation	Rationale Classification
CBS (U.S.)	Banks own 5.79% of the stock The New York banks own 2.56% of the stock Citibank and Bankers Trust each have one director There are 12 indirect interlocks with Manufacturers Hanover Trust and 15 with Chemical New York
GT&E (U.S.)	The stock is widely dispersed Banks own 4.01% of the stock Heavy borrowing
Honeywell (U.S.)	The stock is dispersed Citibank is the second largest shareholder with 2.2% Banks own 7.55% of the stock The New York banks own 4.2% of the stock Five banks have seven directors
IT&T (U.S.)	The stock is dispersed Morgan is the largest shareholder with 2.13% Banks own 8.39% of the stock The New York banks own 4.65% of the stock Citibank has one director There is a close link with investment banker Lazard Frères
Ogilvy & Mather (U.S.)	Chase Manhattan is the second largest shareholder with 3.66% of the stock
NCR (U.S.)	Banks own over 10% The New York banks own 3.26% of the stock Citibank has 2 directors Moderate to heavy borrowing
TRW (U.S.)	Banks hold over 20% of the stock and vote 9.4% of the stock Moderate to heavy borrower

5. Category: Miscellaneous

Corporation	Rationale Classification
AEG/Telefunken (F.R.G.)	Control unidentified
Reed International (U.K.)	Control unidentified
EMI (U.K.)	Control unidentified
Reuters (U.K.)	Large institutional holdings by Press Associations The Press Association (representing provincial newspapers of the U.K. and the newspapers of Ireland) owns 41.7% The Newspaper Publishers Association (representing the U.K. national newspapers) owns 41.7% The Australian Associated Press owns 13.9% The New Zealand Press Association owns 2.7%

Table 47 (continued)

Corporation	Rationale Classification
AFP (F.R.)	A cooperative with the clients being responsible for the administration French mass media and the French government are key clients
Associated Press (U.S.)	Ownership by members: U.S. news media
UPI (U.S.)	Largest shareholder is Scripps Howard newspapers
Control Data (U.S.)	Control unidentified
Lockheed (U.S.)	Control shared between lead suppliers of private funds and the military
20th Century Fox (U.S.)	Large institutional nonfinancial investors
Warner Communications (U.S.)	Control unidentified
RCA (U.S.)	Control unidentified RCA is a major defense contractor
Singer (U.S.)	Control unidentified
J.W. Thompson (U.S.)	Large institutional investor—the JWT Retirement Plan owns 8.6% of the voting stock

Table 48
Centers of Financial Control in the Information Industry

Banks/Banking Groups	Significant Links in Home Country With:	Involvement in Foreign Country With:
CHASE GROUP (Chase Manhattan & Chemical New York)	Sperry Rand IBM AT&T CBS Ogilvy & Mather	Fujitsu Hitachi Toshiba Nippon Electric
MORGAN GROUP (J.P. Morgan & Bankers Trust)	General Electric IBM IT&T ABC Burroughs Washington Post Disney Productions McGraw Hill McDonnell Douglas	CGE Nippon Electric Hitachi
CITIBANK	General Electric IBM	Hitachi Nippon Electric
DEUTSCHE BANK	Siemens Nixdorf	Reed International NCR Toshiba
PARIBAS	Hachette Thomson-Brandt	20th Century Fox
SUMITOMO BANK	Matsushita Nippon Electric Sanyo	IBM
DAI ICHI KANGYO BANK	Hitachi Fujitsu	IBM
MITSUI BANK	Toshiba	IBM

To these eight banks/banking groups have to be added: the Swiss Union de Banque Suisse with significant links to Hachette and involvement with Litton, Honeywell, NCR, General Electric, Bosch, Siemens, and Hitachi; and the investment banking house Larard Frères significantly linked to S. Pearson, EMI and IT&T.

Appendices

APPENDIX I

Net Income As % of Total Sales/Operating Revenues

Corporation	1976	1979
AT&T	11.6	12.5
IBM	14.7	13.2
Philips	1.8	1.9
Matsushita	3.8	4.1
RCA	3.3	3.8
Xerox	8.1	8.0
IT&T	4.2	2.2
International Paper	7.2	11.4
General Electric	5.9	6.3
Siemens	2.7	2.4
AEG-Telefunken	3.0	8.3
Hitachi	3.0	3.8
Reed	1.0	2.0
Sperry Rand	4.5	5.4
CBS	7.4	5.5
Rockwell	2.4	4.0
Thomson-Brandt	1.2	0.9
NCR	4.1	7.8
Burroughs	9.9	11.0
Nippon Electric	0.9	1.0
Sony	6.8	2.8
Rank Xerox	13.1	10.3
Control Data	3.6	5.5
Honeywell	4.5	6.2
ABC	5.3	7.8
Ericsson	2.0	2.1
EMI	3.6	0.02
Lockheed	1.2	1.4
Fujitsu	2.3	2.6
Litton	0.8	4.6
Northern Telecom	6.9	6.0
TRW	4.5	4.3
Grundig	5.9	3.0
Plessey	4.0	4.3
CGE	1.4	0.9
Bertelsmann	0.7	0.3
Warner Communications	7.4	12.2
Time Inc.	6.5	5.7
Digital Equipment	10.0	9.9
MCA	11.2	14.1
Texas Instruments	5.9	5.4
CII-Honeywell Bull	2.8	4.1

APPENDIX I (continued)

Corporation	1976	1979
Gulf & Western	5.9	4.3
McDonnell Douglas	3.1	2.8
ICL	4.3	4.4
McGraw Hill	6.9	8.7
Sanyo	3.0	3.0
LTV	0.7	2.2
New York Times	4.9	5.6
Toshiba	0.3	1.4
Washington Post	6.5	5.9
20th Century Fox	3.0	8.7
Columbia Pictures	3.4	6.4
Thomson Organization	2.0	5.9
S. Pearson	6.1	7.3
Playboy	1.0	3.1
Hewlett Packard	8.2	8.6

APPENDIX II

PROJECT:

BANKING AND INTERNATIONAL COMMUNICATIONS

QUESTIONNAIRE

(After processing, the results of
the study will be sent to you).

1) Name and address of bank:

2) Total amount (per annum) spent for communication facilities
(inclusive of equipment and services):

3) What kind of communication equipment is used by the bank
(e.g., telex, computer):

4) For which transmissions are communication facilities mainly
used (e.g., funds transfer, credit letters):

5) Is an approximation available of the total volume of data that
flows through your communication channels (e.g., number
of transmissions per day):

6) Is your bank involved in any other communications network
outside SWIFT. If so, could you provide some documentation.

APPENDIX II (continued)

PROJECT:

BANKING AND INTERNATIONAL COMMUNICATIONS

7) Does your bank have any public information services (e.g., regular publications, data bank access):

8) Does income from such services constitute any important percentage of the bank's total revenues:

COLUMBIA PICTURES INDUSTRIES INC
TOTAL VOTES: 7,924,000

Business Lines	Percent Op Rev	Percent Income

Stock Class	Shares (000's)	Votes/Share	Votes (000's)	Holders of Record

Counsel/Wash Rep	Serv Fee (000) Year

Investment Bank	Service

Accountant

Voting Concentration

TOP 5 SHAREHOLDERS VOTE 22.05% OF STOCK
TOP 10 SHAREHOLDERS VOTE 22.56% OF STOCK
TOP 15 SHAREHOLDERS VOTE 22.56% OF STOCK
TOP 20 SHAREHOLDERS VOTE 22.56% OF STOCK

	MANAGED HOLDINGS		
	Voting Power		Total Managed Holdings
PRINCIPAL STOCKHOLDERS	Number of Votes	% Total Votes	
1. Rosenhaus, Matthew B & Family#	714,067M	9.01	714,067M
2. Kerkorian, Kirk	492,337M	6.21	492,337M
3. Allen Family Interests#	413,300C	5.22	413,300C
Allen, Herbert E (249500)			
Allen & Co (100500)			
Kramer, Irwin H & Family (63300)			
4. Jaffe, Leo#	91,858C	1.16	91,858C
5. Hirschfield, Alan J & Family#	35,700C	.44	35,700C
6. Strauss, Robert#	23,000C	.28	23,000C
7. Tedlow, Samuel L#	17,505C	.21	17,505C
TOTALS	1,787,767	22.56%	1,787,767

CONTROL DATA CORP
TOTAL VOTES: 16,748,661

PRINCIPAL STOCKHOLDERS	MANAGED HOLDINGS Voting Power Number of Votes	% Total Votes	Total Managed Holdings
1. Norris, William C & Family#	396,307E	2.37	396,307E
2. Capital Research & Management Co*	320,000	1.91	320,000
Investment Company Of America (320000)			
3. Robeco (Holland)	200,000	1.19	200,000
Rolinco (200000)			
4. Pioneer Western Corp<	196,000	1.17	196,000
Pioneering Management Corp*			
Pioneer Fund Inc (196000)			
5. Keystone Custodian Funds Inc*	124,600	.73	124,600
Keystone Speculative Comm St-Ks4 (124600)			
6. Mathers & Co Inc*	120,000	.71	120,000
Mathers Fund (120000)			
7. Sears Roebuck & Co	101,000	.59	101,000
Allstate Insurance Co (101000)			
8. American National Financial Corp<	100,000	.59	100,000
American National Insur Co (75000)			
Securities Management & Research Corp*			
American National Growth Fund (25000)			
9. Gates Rubber Co<	100,000	.59	100,000
Financial Programs Inc*			
Financial Industrial Fund Inc (100000)			
10. Prudential Insurance Co Of Am	95,000	.56	95,000
11. Minnesota State Board Of Investment	81,000	.47	81,000
12. Morgan Guaranty Trust Co Of NY	72,019	.42	71,980
13. Wellington Management Co*	68,000	.40	68,000
Windsor Fund (68000)			
14. California, University Of	63,113B	.37	63,113B
15. Harris Trust & Savings Bank	59,150	.34	59,150
16. Bankamerica Corp<	45,552	.26	45,748
17. Common Fund	20,000B	.11	20,000
18. Manufacturers National Bank Of Detroit	2,845	.01	96,045
19. First Pennsylvania Bank NA	225	-	47,511
TOTALS	2,164,811	12.93%	2,305,454

Business Lines — Percent Op Rev, Percent Income

Stock Class — Shares (000's), Votes/Share, Votes (000's), Holders of Record

Counsel/Wash Rep — Serv Fee (000), Year

Investment Bank — Service

Accountant

Voting Concentration
TOP 5 SHAREHOLDERS VOTE 7.39% OF STOCK
TOP 10 SHAREHOLDERS VOTE 10.47% OF STOCK
TOP 15 SHAREHOLDERS VOTE 12.52% OF STOCK
TOP 20 SHAREHOLDERS VOTE 12.93% OF STOCK

INTERPUBLIC GROUP OF COS
TOTAL VOTES: 2,291,805

Business Lines — Percent Op Rev — Percent Income

Stock Class — Shares (000's) — Votes/Share — Votes (000's) — Holders of Record

Counsel/Wash Rep — Serv Fee (000) Year

Investment Bank — Service

Accountant

Voting Concentration

TOP 5 SHAREHOLDERS VOTE 30.91% OF STOCK
TOP 10 SHAREHOLDERS VOTE 38.78% OF STOCK
TOP 15 SHAREHOLDERS VOTE 42.49% OF STOCK
TOP 20 SHAREHOLDERS VOTE 44.86% OF STOCK

| | MANAGED HOLDINGS | | |
| | Voting Power | | |
PRINCIPAL STOCKHOLDERS	Number of Votes	% Total Votes	Total Managed Holdings
1. Buffett, Warren E Family Interests	442,100E	19.29	442,100E
Berkshire Hathaway Inc (442100)			
2. Capital Research & Management Co*	85,000	3.71	85,000
Amcap Fund Inc (30000)			
New Perspective Fund Inc (55000)			
3. R C S Management Co Inc*	85,000	3.71	85,000
Sequoia Fund (85000)			
4. Healy, Robert E#	48,307E	2.11	48,307E
Wellington Management Co*			
5. Gemini Fund Inc (48100)	48,100	2.10	48,100
6. Plowe, Elliott W#	43,568E	1.90	43,568E
7. Gilliat, Neal & Family#	41,829E	1.83	41,829E
8. Power Corp-Investors Group Of Canada<	36,800	1.61	36,800
Great-West Life Insurance Co (36800)			
9. Foley, Paul#	33,432E	1.46	33,432E
10. Criteron Management Corp	24,600	1.07	24,600
Funds Inc*			
Impact Fund Inc (24600)			
11. Adams, Thomas B#	23,333E	1.02	23,333E
12. Western Bancorporation<	18,800	.81	18,800
First National Bank Of Oregon (18800)			
13. Spielvogel, Carl#	16,583E	.71	16,583E
14. First National Bank Of Boston	13,500	.58	13,500
15. Rainer National Bank	12,600	.55	12,600
16. Bankamerica Corp<	12,000	.51	12,000
17. Columbia Management Co*	12,000	.51	12,000
Columbia Growth Fund Inc (12000)			
18. Kummel, Eugene H#	10,532E	.45	10,532E
19. Mcnamara, J Donald#	10,111E	.43	10,111E
20. AGF Management Ltd* (Canada)	9,700	.41	9,700
AGF Special Fund Ltd (9700)			
21. Hogan, William J & Family#	6,333E	.27	6,333E
22. James, Robert L#	6,647E	.25	6,647E
23. Citizens & Southern National Bank (Atlanta)	4,600	.19	4,600
24. Harris Trust & Savings Bank	-		19,800
TOTALS	1,045,075	45.60%	1,064,875

APPENDIX III (continued)

WASHINGTON POST CO
TOTAL VOTES: 15908000

| | MANAGED HOLDINGS | | |
| | Investment Authority | | |
PRINCIPAL STOCKHOLDERS	Number of Shares	% of Total	Voting Power
1. Graham Family Interests#	3,815,666	23.99	5,332,332
Graham, Katherine Meyer & Assoc (1452546)			
Graham, Donald E Fam & Assoc (1202668)			
Graham, William W (165644)			
Weymouth, Elizabeth Graham (144808)			
Meyer, Eugene Iii & Assoc (800000)			
Sweeterman, John W (40000)			
2. Morgan (J P) & Co Inc<	1,950,000	12.26	1,950,000
3. Buffet, Warren E Family Interests#	1,868,000	11.74	-
Berkshire Hathaway Inc (1868000)			
4. American Security Corp (D C)	943,000	5.93	550,690
5. Oregon Public Employees Retir System	676,000L	4.25	676,000L
6. First Manhattan Co	621,757	3.91	202,676
7. Ruane Cunniff & Co Inc	571,440	3.59	260,000
8. First Northwestern Trust Co of Neb	512,260	3.22	512,260
9. Mackay-Shields Financial Corp	407,400	2.56	407,400
10. Scudder Stevens & Clark Co*	262,560	1.65	250,000
11. R C S Management Co Inc*	260,000	1.63	260,000
Sequoia Fund (260000)			
12. First Investors Corp*	126,500	.79	126,500
13. Travelers Corp<	112,000	.69	112,000
14. Washington Post Co	105,982	.66	105,982
Newsweek Employees Savings Plan (105982)			
15. Meagher, Mark J#	86,000	.53	86,000
16. Columbia Management Co*	78,200	.48	78,200
17. Chaseman, Joel#	40,400	.25	40,400
18. Campbell, Robert D#	36,000	.22	36,000
TOTALS	12,473,165	78.41%	10,986,440

	Percent Op Rev	Percent Income
Business Lines		

	Shares (000's)	Votes/ Share	Votes (000's)	Holders of Record
Stock Class				

	Serv	Fee (000)	Year
Counsel/Wash Rep			

	Service
Investment Bank	

Accountant

Concentration

TOP 5 HOLDERS CONTROL 58 16% OF STOCK
TOP 10 HOLDERS CONTROL 73 10% OF STOCK
TOP 15 HOLDERS CONTROL 77 44% OF STOCK
TOP 20 HOLDERS CONTROL 78 41% OF STOCK

CDEProfile

153

Bibliography

Aronson, J. D., *Money and Power: Banks and the World Monetary System,* Sage, Beverly Hills, California, 1977, 224 pp.

Bächlin, P., *Ekonomiese geschiedenis van de film,* (Economic history of the film), Socialistische Uitgeverij, Nijmegen, 1977, 195 pp.

Bagdikian, B. H., *The Information Machines,* Harper & Row, New York, 1971, 359 pp.

Barnet, R. J., and Müller, R. E., *Global Reach,* Simon & Schuster, New York, 1974, 508 pp.

Barnouw, E., *The Tube of Plenty,* Oxford University Press, New York, 1975, 518 pp.

Barnouw, E., *The Sponsor,* Oxford University Press, New York, 1978, 220 pp.

Baum, D. J., and Stiles, N. B. *The Silent Partners: Institutional Investors and Corporate Control,* Syracuse University Press, Syracuse, New York, 1905, 176 pp.

Becker, J., "The Paper Crisis in Peripheral Capitalism." In *Peace and the Sciences,* International Institute for Peace, Vol. 1, Vienna, 1978, pp. 12-21.

Bell, D., "Communications Technology—For Better or For Worse." *Harvard Business Review,* Vol. 57, No. 3, May-June 1979, pp. 20-42.

Benedetti, F. de, "The Impact of Electronic Technology in the Office." Paper for the Conference Tomorrow in World Electronics, London, March, 1979.

Benton, J. B., "Electronic Funds Transfer: Pitfalls and Payoffs." *Harvard Business Review,* Vol. 55, No. 4, July-Aug., 1977, pp. 16-17.

Bergman, R., "Die monopolistische Organisation der Nachrichtenagenturen in den Hauptländer des Imperialismus und die Konsequenzen für den Nachrichteninhalt,' (The monopolistic organization of the news agencies in the metropoles of imperialism and the consequences for the newscontent). In "Report Der Anteil der Massenmedien bei der Herausbildung des Bewusstseins in der sich wandelnden Welt," 9th General Assembly and Scientific Conference of the

155

International Association for Mass Communication Research, Leipzig, 1974, pp. 3-10.

Berle, A. A., and Means, G., *The Modern Corporation and Private Property*, Macmillan, New York, 1932, 396 pp.

Bernstein, P. W., "Here Come the Superagencies," *Fortune*, Vol. 100, No. 2, Aug. 27, 1979, pp. 46-54.

Boyd Barrett, O., "The World-Wide Agencies: Strengths and Limitations. In "Report Der Anteil der Massenmedien bei der Herausbildung des Bewusstseins in der sich wandelnden Welt," 9th General Assembly and Scientific Conference of the International Association for Mass Communication Research, Leipzig, 1974, pp. 11-16.

Boyd Barrett, O., "The Global News Wholesalers." In Gerbner, G., (ed.), *Mass Media Policies in Changing Cultures*, Wiley & Sons, New York, 1977, pp. 13-20.

Boyd Barrett, O., "Media Imperialism: Towards an International Framework for the Analysis of Media Systems." In Curran, J., Gurevitch, M., and Woollacott, J., (eds.), *Mass Communication and Society*, Edward Arnold, London, 1977, pp. 116-135.

Brown, L., *Television, the Business Behind the Box*, Harcourt, Brace, Jovanovich, New York, 1971, 374 pp.

Brown, M. B., *The Economics of Imperialism*, Penguin, Harmondsworth, England, 1974, 301 pp.

Cardona, E. de, "Multinational Television," *Journal of Communication*, Vol. 25, No. 2, Spring 1975, pp. 122-127.

CDE Handbook, Banking & Finance, New York, 1980, 57 pp.

Chamoux, J. P., *L'information sans frontieres* (Information without borders), La Documentation Francaise, Paris, 1980, 179 pp.

Chapple, S., and Garofalo, R., *Rock 'n Roll is Here to Pay*, Nelson Hall, Chicago, 1977, 354 pp.

Cherry, C., *World Communication: Threat or Promise?* Rev. ed., Wiley, New York, 1978, 229 pp.

Clement, M. *The Canadian Corporate Elite*, McClelland and Stewart, Toronto, 1975, 479 pp.

Cohen, R. B., "Lending by Transnational Banks and Other Financial Institutions to Transnational Corporations," Report to the United Nations Centre on Transnational Corporations, New York, 1979.

Collier, P., and Horowitz, D., *The Rockefellers*, Signet Book, New York, 1976, 774 pp.

Compaine, B. M., (ed.), *Who Owns the Media?* Harmony Books, New York, 1979, 368 pp.

Cook, D. A., "Your Money and Your Life," *Columbia Journalism Review*, Vol. 18, July-Aug. 1979, pp. 64-66.

Cruise O'Brien, R., "Domination and Dependence in Mass Communication: Implications for the Use of Broadcasting in Developing Countries," Institute of Development Studies, Sussex, England, 1974, 11 pp.

Cruise O'Brien, R., "Technological Factors in International Communication," Paper for the 11th General Assembly and Scientific Conference of the International Association for Mass Communciation Research, Warsaw, 1978.

Cruise, O'Brien, R., "Mass Media Ownership," International Commission for the Study of Communication Problems, Paper No. 46, UNESCO, Paris, 1979, 18 pp.

Desmond, R. W., *The Information Process: World News Reporting to the Twentieth Century,* University of Iowa Press, Iowa City, Iowa, 1978, 495 pp.

Diederichs, H. H., *Konzentration in den Massenmedien,* Carl Hanser Verlag, Munich, Germany, 1973, 247 pp.

Dizard, W., "Television's Global Networks." In Fischer, H. D. and Merrill, J. C., *International and Intercultural Communication,* Rev. 2nd ed., Hastings House, New York, 1978, pp. 83-89.

Dodwell Marketing Consultants, *Industrial Groupings in Japan,* rev. ed., 1978, 466 pp.

Dost, M., Hopf, F., and Kluge, A., *Filmwirtschaft in der BRD und Europa,* Carl Hanser Verlag, Munich, Germany, 1973.

Dreier, P., and Weinberg, S., "Interlocking Directorates, Newspaper Companies, and the Institutions They Cover," *Columbia Journalism Review,* Vol. 18, Nov.-Dec. 1979, pp. 51-68.

Dunning, J. H., and Pearce, R. B., "Profitability and Performance of the World's Largest Industrial Companies," *Financial Times,* London, 1975, p. 48.

Engberg, O., "The Way to the Information Society," *Information Privacy,* Vol. 1, No. 7, Sept. 1979, pp. 282-289.

Evans, C., *The Mighty Micro,* Gollancz, London, 1979, 255 pp.

Ewen, S., "The Bribe of Frankenstein," *Journal of Communications,* Vol. 29, No. 4, Autumn 1979, pp. 12-19.

Fajnzylber, F., and Tarragó, T. M., *Las empresas transnacionales,* Fondo de Cultura Económica, Mexico, 1976, 423 pp.

"The Film Council." In A. Mattelart and S. Siegelaub, (Eds.), *Communication and Class Struggle, An Anthology,* Vol. I, International General, New York; International Mass-Media Research Center, Bagnolet, France, 1979, pp. 252-259.

Freese, J., International Data Flow, StudentlitteraturAB, Lund, Sweden, 1979, 86 pp.

Frutkin, A. W., "Space Communications and the Developing Countries." In Gerbner, G., Melody, W. H., and Gross, L. P., *Communications Technology and Social Policy,* Wiley & Sons, New York, 1973, pp. 369-380.

Garnham, N., "Towards a Political Economy of Mass Communication," Paper for the 11th General Assembly and Scientific Conference of the International Association for Mass Communication Research, Warsaw, 1978, 59 pp.

Garnham, N., "The Economics of the U.S. Motion Picture Industry," Report for the Commission of the European Communities, Strasbourg, 1980, 41 pp.

Golding, P., "The International Media and the Political Economy of Publishing, *Library Trends,* Vol. 26, Spring, 1978, pp. 453-467.

Golding, P., and Murdock, G., "Capitalism, Communication and Class Relations." In Curran, J., Gurevitch, M., and Woolacott, J. *Mass Communication and Society,* Edward Arnold, London, 1977, pp. 12-43.

Gonzalez Manet, E., *Informatización de la Sociedad: Nueve Forma de Dependencia?* (Informatization of the society: A new form of dependence?), Instituto Latinoamericano de Estudios Transnacionales, Mexico City, 1970, (Dec/D/59/), 60 pp.

Gonzalez Manet, E., "The International Information System—A Critical Analysis," Paper for the 12th General Assembly and Scientific Conference of the International Association for Mass Communication Research, Caracas, Aug., 1980, 28 pp.

Gorostiago, X., *Los Banqueros del Imperio,* Editorial Universitaria Centro Americana, Costa Rica, 1978, 113 pp.

Gronow, P., "The Record Industry, Multinational Corporations and National Music Traditions," Paper for International Institute for Music, Dance and Theatre in the Audiovisual Media, Vienna, 1975.

Gronow, P., "Systemes de Filtrage et de Promotion dans l'Industrie du Disque et leurs Consequences pour les Artistes et le Public," (Promotional systems in the record industry and their consequences for the artists and the public), Paper for the Council of Europe Conference on "The State's Role vis-a-vis Culture," Strasbourg, April, 1980, 14 pp.

Guback, T. H., "Film as International Business," *Journal of Communication*, Vol. 24, No. 1, Winter 1974, pp. 90-101.

Guback, T. H., "Hollywood's World Market." In Balio, T., (ed.), *The American Film Industry*, University of Wisconsin Press, Madison, 1976, pp. 387-409.

Guback, T. H., "The International Film Industry." In Gerbner, G. (ed.) *Mass Media Policies in Changing Cultures*, Wiley & Sons, New York, 1977, pp. 21-40.

Guback, T. H., "Notes on Imperialism and the Film Industry," University of Illinois, Institute of Communication Research, Urbana, 1978, 14 pp.

Guback, T. H., "Theatrical Film." In B. Compaine (ed.) *Who Owns the Media*, Harmony Books, New York, 1979, pp. 179-249.

Guback, T. H., "International Circulation of Theatrical Motion Pictures and Television Programming," Paper for the Conference World Communications: Decisions for the Eighties, Annenberg School of Communications, Philadelphia, May 1980, 15 pp.

Guzzardi, W., "The Great World Telephone War," *Fortune*, Vol. 96, No. 2, Aug. 1977, pp. 142-154.

Halberstam, D., *The Powers That Be*, A. A. Knopf, New York, 1979, 771 pp.

Hamelink, C. J., "De Multinationals en de Bewustzijnsindustrie," (The multinationals and the consciousness-industry), *Massacommunicatie*, Vol. 4, No. 2, June, 1976, pp. 65-71.

Hamelink, C. J., "Transnationale Gesellschaften und internationale Kommunikationsstrukturen," (Transnational corporations and structures of international communication), *Der Ueberblick*, No. 4, December, 1976, pp. 29-32.

Hamelink, C. J., *The Corporate Village*, IDOC, Rome, 1977, 233 pp.

Hamelink, C. J., "Dal Grande Villaggio al Grande Mercate," (From big village to big market), *IDOC Internazionale*, No. 5, Rome, May 1977, pp. 10-16.

Hamelink, C. J., *De Mythe van de Vrije Informatie*, (The myth of the freedom of information), Anthos, Baarn, 1978, 156 pp.

Hamelink, C. J., "Imperialism of Satellite Technology," *WACC/Journal*, No. 1, 1979, pp. 13-17.

Hamelink, C. J., "Informatica en een Nieuwe Informatie Orde," *Massacommunicatie*, Vol. 7, No. 3, 1979, pp. 90-103.

Hamelink, C. J., (ed.), *Communication in the Eighties, A Reader on the McBride Report*, IDOC, Rome 1980, 61 pp.

Hamelink, C. J., *De Computersamenleving*, (The Computersociety) Anthos, Baarn, 1980, 120 pp.

Hamelink, C. J., "International Finance and the Information Industry," Paper for the Conference World Communications: Decisions for the Eighties, Annenberg School of Communications, Philadelphia, May, 1980, 15 pp.

Hamelink, C. J., *Cultural Autonomy in Global Communications*, Longman, New York, (forthcoming).

Helmers, H. M., Mokken, R. J., Plijter, R. C. and Stokman, F. N., *Graven naar Macht*, (Digging for power), Van Gennep, Amsterdam, 1975, 487 pp.

Hester, A., 'International news agencies." In Wells, A. (ed.), *Mass Communication: A World View*, National Press Books, Palo Alto, California, 1974.

Hexelscheider, E. and Kleinwächter, W., "Die expansion internationaler journalistischer Konzerne und daraus erwachsende Probleme für die internationalen Beziehunge der Gegenwart." In "Report Der Anteil der Massenmedien bei der Herausbildung des Bewusstseins in der sich wandelnden Welt," 9th General Assembly and Scientific Conference of the International Association for Mass Communication Research, Leipzip, 1974, pp. 49-53.

Hilferding, R., *Das Finanzkapital*, Part I and II, Europäische Verlagsanstalt, Frankfurt, 1968, 244 pp. and 313 pp.

Höhne, H., *Report über Nachrichtenagenturen*, (Report on newsagencies), Part 1 and 2, Nomos, Baden-Baden, 1977. (Part 1: Die Situation auf den Nachrichtenmärkten der Welt (The Situation on the world newsmarkets), 224 pp., Part 2: Die Geschichte der Nachricht und ihre Verbreiter (The history of news and its distributors), 181 pp.

Hogrebe, E. F. M., "Dangers and Opportunities of Digital Communication Media," Report for the Instituto Latinoamericano de Estudios Transnacionales, Mexico City, April 1980.

Huet, A., etal, *Capitalisme et Industries Culturelles*, Presses Universitaires de Grenoble, Grenoble, France, 1977, 198 pp.

International Commission for the Study of Communication Problems, "The World of News Agencies," Paper 11, UNESCO, Paris, 1978.

International Commission for the Study of Communication Problems, *Many Voices, One World*, UNESCO, Paris, 1980, 312 pp.

James, T. E., Jr., "Motion Picture Industry Data," mimeo, San Francisco, 1980, 50 pp.

Janus, N., and Roncagliolo, R., "A Survey of the Transnational Structure of the Mass Media and Advertising," Report for the UN Centre on Transnational Corporations, Mexico, July 1978, 350 pp.

Jensen, M. C., *The Financiers*, Weybright and Talley, New York, 1976, 340 pp.

Junne, G., "Multinational Banks, The State and International Integration." In K. von Beyme (ed.), *German Political Systems*, Sage, London, 1976, pp. 117-137.

Jussawalla, M., "The Economics of International Communication," *Third World Quarterly*, Vol. 1, No. 3, July 1979, pp. 87-94.

Kimbel, D., "An Assessment of the Computer-Telecommunications Complex in Europe, Japan, and North America." In Gerbner, G., Melody, W. H., and Gross, L. P., (eds.), *Communications Technology and Social Policy*, Wiley & Sons, New York, 1973, pp. 147-164.

Kleinwächter, W., and Raaz, F., "Imperialistische Aussenpropaganda im Zwang der Anpassung" (Imperialist Foreign Propaganda in the Service of Adaptation), *Deutsche Aussenpolitik*, No. 1, Berlin, 1979, pp. 92-108.

Kotz, D. M., *Bank Control of Large Corporations in the United States*, University of California Press, Berkeley, California, 1978, 217 pp.

Lavey, W. G., *Toward a Quantification of the Information/Communication Industries*, Publication Program on Information Technologies and Public Policy, Harvard University, Cambridge, Massachusetts, May 1974, 114 pp.

Levine, J., "Interbank Touts Clout for Women," *Advertising Age*, June 1979, pp. 1, 80.

Mattelart, A., "Modern Communication Technology and New Facets of Cultural Imperialism, *Instant Research on Peace and Violence,* Tampere Peace Research Institute, Vol. 1, 1973, Tampere, Finland, pp. 9-26.

Mattelart, A., "Cultural Imperialism in the Multinationals' Age," *Instant Research on Peace and Violence,* Tampere Peace Research Institute, Vol. 6, No. 4, 1976, pp. 160-174.

Mattelart, A., *Multinationales et Systèmes de Communication,* Editions Anthropos, Paris, 1976, 391 pp.

Mattelart, A., "Die eigentlichen Pädagogen unserer Zeit," (The real educators of our time), In Becker, J., *Free Flow of Information,* Gemeinschattswerk der Evangelischen Publizistik, Frankfurt, 1979, No. 8, pp. 101-131.

Mattelart, A., "The Geopolitics of Paper," In Mattelart, A., and Siegelaub, S., (eds.), *Communication and Class Struggle, An Anthology,* Vol. I: "Capitalism, Imperialism," International General, New York; International Mass Media Research Center, Bagnolet, France, 1979, pp. 305-308.

Mattelart, A., *The Multinational Corporations and the Control of Culture: The Ideological Apparatus of Imperialism,* Harvester Press, Atlantic Highlands, New Jersey, 1979.

Mattelart, A., "The Satellite Systems," In Mattelart, A. and Siegelaub, S., (eds.), *Communication and Class Struggle, An Anthology,* Vol I: " Capitalism, Imperialism," International General, New York; International Mass Media Research Center, Bagnolet, France, 1979, pp. 328-331.

McAnany, E. G., "Does Information Really Work?" *Journal of Communications,* Vol. 28, No. 1, Winter 1978, pp. 84-90.

Meier, W., and Schanne, M., "Nachrichtenagenturen und globales Schichtungssystem," (Newsagencies and global hierarchical system), *Publizistik,* Vol. 2, 1979, pp. 213-222.

Meier, W., and Schanne, M., "Nachrichtenagenturen in internationalen System" (Newsagencies in the international system), Publizistisches Seminar der Universität Zürich, 1980, 156 pp.

Mestrovic, M., "Information, Economics and Development," Paper for the International Institute of Communications Annual Conference, Sept. 1978, Dubrovnik.

Meyer, G. de, *De populaire Muziekindustrie,* (The popular music industry), Centrum voor Communicatiewetenschappen, Leuven, 1979.

Monaco, J., *Media Culture,* Delta Book, New York, 1978, 335 pp.

Mosco, V., and Herman, A., "Radical Theory and Electronic Media," Paper for the Annual Meeting of the American Sociological Association, New York, Aug. 1980, 46 pp.

Mowlana, H., "The Multinational Corporation and the Diffusion of Technology." In Said, A. A., and Simmons, L. R., *The New Sovereigns-Multinational Corporations as World Powers,* Prentice Hall, Englewood Cliffs, New Jersey, 1975, pp. 77-90.

Murdock, G., "Mass Media and the Class Structure—An Exploratory Study in Britain," Report, Centre for Mass Communication Research, Leicester, June 1979, 27 pp.

Nabudere, D., *The Political Economy of Imperialism,* Zed Press, London, 1977, 301 pp.

Nora, S., and Minc, A., *L'Informatisation de la Société,* La Documentation Francaise, Paris, 1978, 162 pp.

Norman, C., "Knowledge and Power: The Global Research and Development Budget." *Worldwatch Paper* No. 31, July 1979, 56 pp.

Oettinger, A. G., and Shapiro, P. D., *Information Industries in the United States*, Harvard University Program on Information Resources Policy, Cambridge, Massachusetts, 1975, 10 pp.

Organisation for Economic Cooperation and Development, *Impact of Multinational Enterprises on National Scientific and Technical Capacities*, OECD Directorate for Science, Technology and Industry, Paris, Dec. 1977.

P.A. Management Consultants' Report, *Informatics in European Banks in 1980*, Brussels, 1980.

Pearce, A., "Telematics Market Heating Up," *Telecommunications*, May, 1980, pp. 10-16.

Peron, R., "The Record Industry," In Mattelart, A., and Siegelaub, S., (eds.), *Communication and Class Struggle, An Anthology*, Vol. I: Capitalism, Imperialism, International General, New York; International Mass Media Research Center, Bagnolet, France, 1979, pp. 292-297.

Pool, I. de S. "International Telecommunications and the Requirements of News Services," Occasional Paper, The Fletcher School of Law and Diplomacy, Edward R. Murrow Center of Public Diplomacy, Tufts University, 1978, 19 pp.

Porat, M. U., *The Information Economy*, Vol. 1 and 2, U.S. Department of Commerce, Office of Telecommunications, May 1977, 250 pp. and 180 pp.

Porat, M. U., "Global Implications of the Information Society," *Journal of Communication*, Vol. 28, No. 1, Winter 1978, pp. 70-80.

Portales, D., "Oligopolizacion y Transnacionalizacion en la Industria de la Communicacion," FLASCO paper, Aug., 1978, 75 pp.

Prives, D., *E.F.T. Policy and Competitive Equality*, Publication Program on Information Technologies and Public Policy, Harvard University, Cambridge, Massachusetts, Jan. 1977, 52 pp.

Radice, H. (ed.), *International Firms and Modern Imperialism*, Penguin, Harmondsworth, England, 1975, 264 pp.

Read, W. H., "Multinational Media," *Foreign Policy*, No. 18, Spring, 1975, pp. 155-167.

Read, W. H., *America's Mass Media Merchants*, John Hopkins University Press, Baltimore, Maryland, 1976, 209 pp.

Reyes Matta, F., *La Evolución Histórica de las Agencias Transnacionales de Noticias haca la Dominación*, (The historical development of the transnational news-agencies towards domination). In La Información en el Neuvo Orden Internacional, Instituto Latinoamericano de Estudios Transnacionales, Mexico City, 1977, pp. 53-66.

Robinson, A., "Metamorphosis in the Media," *Financial Times*, Nov. 18, 1977.

Roncagliolo, R., and Janus, N., "Advertising. Mass Media and Dependency," *Development Dialogue*, No. 1, 1979, Uppsala, Sweden, pp. 81-97.

Rose, S., "The Unexpected Fallout from Electronic Banking," *Fortune*, April 24, 1979, p. 83.

Sampson, A., *The Sovereign State of ITT*, Stein and Day, New York, 1973, 323 pp.

Sarnoff, A. P., "America's Press: Too Much Power for Too Few?" Special Report in *U.S. News & World Report*, Aug. 15, 1977, pp. 27-33.

Sauvant, K. P., and Lavipour, F. G., (eds.), *Controlling Multinational Enterprises*, Campus Verlag, Frankfurt, 1976, 335 pp.

Sieden, M. N., *Who Controls the Mass Media?* Basic Books, New York, 1974, 246 pp.

Schiller, H. I., *Mass Communications and American Empire*, Beacon Press, Boston, 1971, 170 pp.

Schiller, H. I., *The Mind Managers*, Beacon Press, Boston, 1973, 214 pp.

Schiller, H. I., "Advertising and International Communications," *Instant Research on Peace and Violence*, Tampere Peace Research Institute, Vol. 6, No. 4, Tampere, Finland 1976, pp. 175-182.

Schiller, H. I., *Communication and Cultural Domination*, International Arts and Sciences Press, New York, 1976, 126 pp.

Schiller, H. I., "Computer Systems: Power for Whom and for What? *Journal of Communication*, Vol. 28, No. 4, Autumn, 1978, pp. 184-193.

Schiller, H. I., "Communication Accompanies Capital Flows," International Commission for the Study of Communication Problems, Paper 47, UNESCO, Paris, 1979, 13 pp.

Schiller, H. I., "Planetary Resources Information Flows: A New Dimension of Hegemonic Power or Global Social Utility?" Paper for the Conference World Communications: Decisions for the Eighties, Annenberg School of Communications, Philadelphia, May 1980.

Soldofsky, R. M., *Institutional Holdings of Common Stock, 1900-2000*, Bureau of Business Research, University of Michigan, Ann Arbor, 1971, 228 pp.

Somavia, J., "The Transnational Power Structure and International Information," *Development Dialogue*, No. 2, 1976, Uppsala, Sweden, pp. 15-28.

Soramäki, M., and Haarma, J., "The International Music Industry," Preliminary Report, Finnish Broadcasting Corporation, Department of Planning and Research, Helsinski, 1978.

Sparks, W., "The Flow of Information and the New Technology of Money," Address at the Conference on World Communications: Decisions for the Eighties, at the Annenberg School of Communications, Philadelphia, May 1980.

Stanton, R., "The Supply of Television Equipment to Developing Countries," A U.K. case study. Unpublished report, Institute of Development Studies, University of Sussex, 1979.

Sterling, C. H., and Haight, T. R., *The Mass Media: Aspen Institute Guide to Communication Industry Trends*, Praeger, New York, 1978, 457 pp.

Teulings, A., *Philips*, Van Gennep, Amsterdam, 1975, 325 pp.

Toffler, A., *The Third Wave*, Morrow, New York, 1980, 544 pp.

Toussaint, N., *L'Economie de l'Information*, Presse Universitaire de France, 1978, 125 pp.

Tunstall, J., *The Media are American*, Columbia University Press, New York, 1977, 352 pp.

U.S. Department of Commerce, *Current Developments in U.S. International Service Industries*, U.S. Government Printing Office, Washington, D.C., March 1980.

Varis, T., "The Impact of Transnational Corporations on Communication," Working Paper, UNESCO, Paris, 1976.

Varis, T., "The Mass Media Transnational Corporations: An Overall View of Their Operations and Control Options," *Cooperation and Conflict*, Vol. 13, 1978, pp. 193-213.

Väyrynen, R., "Concentration and Internationalization in Banking," *Research Report*, Series D, Department of Political Science, University of Turku, No. 4, 1975.

Veith, R. H., *Multinational Computer Nets*, Lexington Books, Toronto, 1981, 133 pp.

Vernon, R., *Storm Over the Multinationals*, Harvard University Press, Cambridge, Massachusetts, 1977, 260 pp.

Vernon, R., *Sovereignty at Bay*, Basic Books, New York, 1971, 326 pp.

Vignolle, J. P., "Développement Récent des Systèmes Nationaux et Internationaux de Distribution de Disque," (Recent development of national and international distribution systems for records), Paper for the Council of Europe Conference on "The State's Role vis-*a*-vis Culture", Strasbourg, April, 1980, 17 pp.

Wachtel, H. M., *The New Gnomes: Multinational Banks in the Third World*, Transnational Institute, Washington, D.C., 1977, 60 pp.

Williams, R., *Marxism and Literature*, Oxford University Press, Oxford, England, 217 pp.

Worthington, R., "The Cultural Connection: Multinational Corporations and the Mass Media," Paper prepared for the Annual Conference of the Western Political Science Association, San Francisco, April 1976.

Zurkowski, P. G., "The Information Service Environment," Paper prepared for the National Commission on Libraries and Information Science, Washington, D.C., No. 1, 1974.

Author Index

Subject Index